Preparing to

Preparing to Parent Teenagers

Paul Scott-Evans

based on an original idea by
Gerard Kelly and Lowell Sheppard

British Youth for Christ Registered Charity No. 263446.
A company limited by guarantee.
Registered in England, Registration No. 00988200.

alpha

Copyright © 1999 Paul Scott-Evans and
Youth for Christ, PO Box 5254, Halesowen, West Midlands B63 3DG

First published in 1999 by Alpha

05 04 03 02 01 00   7 6 5 4 3 2 1

Alpha is an imprint of Paternoster Publishing,
PO Box 300, Carlisle, Cumbria, CA3 0QS, UK
http://www.paternoster-publishing.com

The right of Paul Scott-Evans to be identified as the
Author of this Work has been asserted by him in accordance with
Copyright, Designs and Patents Act 1988.

British Library Cataloguing in Publication Data
A catalogue record for this book is available from the British Library

ISBN 0-89893-869-5

Unless otherwise stated, Scripture quotations are taken from the
HOLY BIBLE, NEW INTERNATIONAL VERSION
Copyright © 1973, 1978, 1984 by the International Bible Society.
Used by permission of Hodder and Stoughton Limited. All rights reserved.
'NIV' is a registered trademark of the International Bible Society
UK trademark number 1448790

Cover Design by Mainstream, Lancaster
Typeset by WestKey Ltd, Falmouth, Cornwall
Printed in Great Britain by
Caledonian International Book Manufacturing Ltd, Glasgow

Contents

Preface

This book has come out of a series of seminars run by Youth for Christ all over the country. I do not consider myself in any way to be an expert, in fact, writing this book has only served to highlight the mistakes I made. Nor do I consider this book to be a manual on how to be a successful parent, but rather a help and stimulus to parents about to embark on their own journey of parenting teenagers, to find their own way. The wonder is that both my sons, now in their early twenties, survived in the 'together' way they have. I must give the credit to a loving and caring God and a loving and very gracious wife. Val has put up with me for over 28 years, put up with my own mid-life crisis, my uprooting her from her home in South London and touching down in the Midlands and, throughout it all, supported the family and me with patience and good humour. She still laughs at my jokes even though she has heard them many times.

My older son, James, has a quiet approach to life which so contrasts with my own noisy character. At his wedding, his brother, Andy, acting as best man, rather than do the 'hatchet job' everyone had advised, said what he appreciated about James. In doing so, he spoke for all of us in the family. 'What I really like about James,' he said, 'is that you don't have to have a conversation to catch up on all the latest happenings in his life but you can just be with him. James is one of those people to be with.' It is a great asset and one he must have inherited from his mother or from one of his grandparents. James is now working at the very thing he so enjoyed as a teenager: programming computers.

Andy, on the other hand, as the younger brother, has never had to live in the shadow of an articulate older sibling. He did, however, follow James through infant, junior and secondary schools and had to put up with teacher comparisons. Whilst we tried not to compare them and tried not to tell them if we did, Andy had problems in this regard. He has a different temperament and he does like to talk, he is good at it. He now puts it to good effect in the classroom as a teacher and in preaching and leading worship. But at school James appeared quiet and industrious whilst Andy was noisier and, therefore, easier to notice when up to mischief.

Both have allowed me to use stories of their adolescence and have happily added their own anecdotes where appropriate to the text.

I am also grateful to Kingsley and Margaret Dent who have helped me with the project. Their input has been very useful as they have three girls, two at University and one working, which has served to balance my rather male-dominated parenting. Theirs has not been a smooth run either and the insights I have gained from them have helped enormously in writing *Preparing to Parent Teenagers*.

I must mention Colin Piper, Director of South West Youth Ministries and an Associate of YFC. His book, *FAMILIES: Don't You Just Love Them*[1], was reviewed favourably by Andy for YFC's magazine *Into View* and his generosity in allowing me to use his interviews with young people has, I believe, contributed another dimension to *Preparing to Parent Teenagers*.

Finally, I need to mention Gerard Kelly and Lowell Sheppard who came up with the idea of the seminars for preparing to parent teenagers and whose material, written for Youth for Christ, provided the foundation from which this book has been built. I also want to thank Rick Bartlett for his invaluable contributions and encouragement, together with Jenny Baker and Wendy Beech from whom I learnt a lot during the presentation of seminars together. Mia Kellmer Pringle, who was the first director of the National Children's Bureau said, 'Modern parenting is too demanding and complex a task to be performed well merely because we have all once been children.'

My prayer is that this book will help prepare you as parents for the joys and challenges of parenting teenagers. This book is about preparation. C.H. Spurgeon, the great Victorian preacher and teacher, said in his later life that if he had twenty-five years still to live he would spend twenty in preparation. Whilst he was talking about ministry, I believe the principle, if not the time, applies to parenting teenagers. There is no such thing as the perfect parent, any more than there is the perfect child and it is good to know all parents, even the most 'together', have problems from time to time. I am grateful for those friends who stood by Val and me as we rode the white-water rapids with our teenage sons. No amount of reading or listening to others could prepare me for the ride but without them, I know I would have spent more time out of my depth.

Foreword

The breakdown of stable family units is having far-reaching effects on children and parents alike. A recent study, done by the Mental Health Foundation revealed that 1 in 5 children suffer from mental health problems before they are old enough to leave home. Parents trying to juggle home and work, often with no support, find themselves continually 'stressed out'.

Into this arena a book such as, *Preparing to Parent Teenagers* demands to be written. Paul is a friend and colleague and he and his wife Val have been involved in many seminars dealing with this topic and answering the questions of many parents. I am thrilled that in writing this book, they have been willing to share their own struggles as they work out what God has to say about families and how the Bible really can be, 'A light to your path'. They offer some excellent insights and practical advice which can be applied to all families.

The statement, 'There is no place like home' does not mean what it used to. For some children, home is simply a place to stay until they are old enough or angry enough to leave. This is not what God planned and it is up to parents to change things.

Sometimes teenagers need to talk, sometimes they need parents just to be there for them, to enter their world and be vulnerable with them. Sometimes they demand that we ride the rapids with them.

Are you equipped for the journey through the teenage years? Are you willing to sit down, to take stock and to plan ahead? This book could prove an invaluable tool. It will certainly challenge and stimulate you as you discover the joy of understanding what family is really meant to be.

Roy Crowne
National Director of Youth For Christ

Introduction

i. Where we are coming from

Youth for Christ is an international organisation which special-
ises in communicating the Christian faith to young people.
Worldwide, three thousand staff and twenty-five thousand vol-
unteers are involved in diverse programmes aiming to carry the
Good News of Jesus to unreached young people and to disciple
them into the church and to mobilise those young people to reach
their peers.

Our work gives us a special and privileged position in relation
to teenagers. As part of a global organisation, we are aware of the
'big picture' – the changes affecting youth culture throughout the
world and the pressures and influences on young people today.
We have also, as part of our concern for young people, undertaken research into their concerns and conducted a large number
of interviews with teenagers. We also gain insights at the level of
the individual and in counselling and guiding young people, we
are often made painfully aware of their frustrations, their hurts
and their sense of inner need.

From the research and preparation for this book we have seen
trends and changes, of which parents may be unaware but which
have serious effects on their children. From talking with adolescents we have gained anecdotal information on the lives of young
people and heard things they have often not dared to say to their
parents. All this persuades us of two overriding facts:

 i) it is not always easy to bring up teenagers,
ii) it is not impossible to bring up teenagers.

It is a journey fraught with threats and dangers, but rich with re-
wards. Success is not guaranteed – but it is available. We believe
that the parents who are better prepared will be the more effective.

ii. 'The River Wild'

Our approach to this subject has led us to view adolescence as a
journey, which adults and children travel together. We have identified three activities essential to preparing for this journey: you need
to know the landscape, you need to plan the route and you need to
pack for the journey. The journey will be presented in these three
stages, with a last word about the place of faith, hope and love in
these matters.

Our preferred image is not of a road or rail journey, but of a
white-water raft, negotiating the turbulence and fury of a river as
it passes through rapids and tight ravines. Experience tells us that
this image is not over-dramatic: those who have gone before have
testified to the turbulence and fury of the adolescence years. Another image which may be more familiar is that of the roller
coaster. A recent BBC Television series, *The Human Body*, presented by Robert Winston, talked of adolescence as a hormone-
driven biological revolution transforming both minds and bodies.
Horror stories abound of those who didn't make it through, or
whose relationships were badly damaged. There are plenty of success stories too, of the deep bonds of love and friendship forged in
families who have made the journey together, and been united by
the challenge. I like to think that from my own experience as both
a father of two sons now in their twenties and as a youth worker
in my own church, I have the credentials to dare to embark on
such a task as writing a book on preparing to parent teenagers.

As instructors will tell you, in white-water rafting preparation
is everything. Knowing the river ahead, planning a route down it
and packing the right equipment are each life-saving strategies.

We believe the same to be true of parenting through the adolescent years. There are some skills which will be needed only when you hit the rapids. There will be strategies you will only need in emergencies. But preparation – knowing the landscape, planning the route and packing for the journey can and will make all the difference.

A mother of three teenagers said, 'The two most difficult times of life are when you *are* a teenager and when you *have* a teenager!'

Someone has said that nowadays, when a teenager mopes around they call it an identity crisis and the parents spend £5,000 on a psychiatrist. Thirty years ago they spent 50p on a laxative!

We believe that preparation can make this difficult time of life easier, on both sides of the fence!

Stage 1

Knowing the Landscape

Chapter 1

A Secure Base

Michael Howard QC, MP, when he was Home Secretary, spoke at an international conference held in London in February 1994. During his speech he quoted from a paediatrician:

> There were times before I had my own children when I was already advising other people on how to bring up theirs. I thought it was all really quite straightforward. These people who came to see me were in a mess. They weren't normal parents like we would be. Then we had children. Then we were in a mess as well!

He went on to talk about the importance of parent education and how he wished there was a network of services for parents to help them in the emotional, psychological and physical aspects of raising children and especially adolescents. He said that such services should be available to all parents and prospective parents to help them develop self-awareness and self-confidence and improve their capacity to nurture and support their children. He wanted opportunities for practical skills to be learnt in how to manage a home and family.

What we hope to do in Youth for Christ is to play our part in this education. This is why we run parenting seminars and why this book has been produced. Knowing the landscape is vital before setting out on a journey.

Setting out from our house in Bromsgrove, we can, within a few minutes be walking across beautiful Worcestershire farmland with wonderful views of Bredon Hill and the Malverns to the south, and the Clee Hills to the west. The walk is undemanding and takes us through wheat and rape fields following public footpaths. The problem is we always forget that part of the walk goes through a particularly vicious bed of stinging nettles. On warm summer days we always set off in shorts only to regret our foolhardiness when faced with the stingers. Even knowing the landscape and even having gone that way before, still does not prevent us from being caught unprepared.

You will make mistakes on the journey of preparing to parent teenagers but being forewarned is, as they say, being forearmed. We know now that there is a way round the stinging nettles and we tend to go this way, even when we are dressed appropriately to negotiate them.

To get back to the speech by Michael Howard, he gave some helpful principles which are good to take into account as we consider the landscape ahead. I quote five of the principles he mentioned.

> Firstly, there is no single right way of parenting, no blueprint for a perfect family. It is important that diverse family patterns are acknowledged and respected.

This is helpful advice and, like a lot of things, appears common sense. The problem with common sense is it's not very common. So at the outset of the journey it is important to realise that your journey is your own, but this is not to say that you will travel it alone. Furthermore there are guiding principles to help you on your way.

> Secondly, parenting is a continuing process. The development of a parent starts at birth and goes on through early childhood, schooldays, early relationships, committed relationships, committed partnerships, pregnancy, birth, parenthood and grandparenthood.

I have put it that we're on a journey. Simply because my sons are now adults, does not mean I am no longer a parent. When I went through my mid-life crisis, James was at University and Andy was studying for his A levels. I had spent nearly thirty years working in the NatWest Bank and was the Manager at the Leatherhead branch when the struggles began. I felt that banking, which up to that point I had always enjoyed, was no longer for me. Perhaps I had been promoted beyond my capabilities. All I can say is I was heading for a breakdown.

I felt I could not talk about this with Val, I simply could not articulate what I was feeling. The tension in the home must have affected Andy, without doubt it affected Val. My work suffered, I was no longer capable of making decisions and I knew this was leading to disaster unless something broke. Fortunately with the help of some very good and perceptive friends I gradually began to realise that perhaps the struggles were caused by my refusal to obey what I felt God was calling me to do. At first I thought it was to the Baptist ministry and I pursued this possibility with the local superintendent. He told me quite firmly that, at forty-seven, I was too old for the Baptist ministry. That door was very firmly closed.

At the time I was a member of the National Board of Youth for Christ and, after much prayer, I shared with Val that I thought perhaps I should approach YFC to see if there was a vacancy for a person with skills such as mine. Val had been feeling I should make such an approach but had been waiting for me to come to the same conclusion. She often gets there much quicker than I do. I telephoned the National Director who said, 'I have been waiting for this call. God told me that if it was right, you would phone and I was not to do anything. I know it's right for you to join YFC. I have just the job for you. Our General Manager has resigned, so please apply for his position.' I was too old for the Baptists but not too old for a youth organisation. God's sense of humour continues to amaze me!

What happened next was to have a serious effect on our sons. We would have to move to the Midlands, leave our church, our friends and our sons. This was flying the nest in reverse: it's the children who are supposed to leave, not the parents. I am now very fulfilled working for YFC but it has been really hard for our sons. They went through a number of years feeling they no longer had a home.

I tell this story about myself to illustrate the truth that parenting is a continuous process. By moving away from home, children do not suddenly stop being your children. I think it is a mistake to think that now they're off your hands you can redecorate the bedrooms, make plans without having to take them into consideration and wash your hands of the whole parent business. I talk more about this in Chapter 17 but, for now, I think it should be understood that the process goes on after the children have left home.

> Thirdly, all parents need help at some point in their lives, but there are likely to be different needs at different stages and these can be met in different ways.

A constant theme of mine is the need to know to whom you can turn for help. In the nuclear family, grandparents are often a source of readily available wisdom, but we found that older friends whose children were now adults, were a very helpful resource. Everyone acknowledges they require help at some point, so I suggest that you think now about who you can turn to when the need arises.

> Fourthly, parenting is not simply a matter of child-rearing; it is a constant interaction between parents and children, both of whom are continually developing.

I cover this principle in Chapter 5, but I know from my own experience that what I thought was a fairly simple task, that of child-rearing, was made so much more complicated by my own personal development. No one stands still and, as John Donne wrote in the seventeenth century, 'No man is an island, entire of itself', we all interact and we are all changing.

> The fifth principle is about self-confidence and self-worth. The ability to parent reflects each individual's level of self-confidence and self-worth.

You may feel it is not very helpful to include self-confidence and self-worth in a list of principles about parent education and knowing the landscape through which you, as a parent will have to travel. After all, can these things be learnt or taught? The problem with us as human beings is that none of us is born with knowledge. Everyone of us has a brain which is, in effect, a computer with no programme. All of life has been programming our brains, our computers and, if we have been taught by our parents that we can be confident in who we are, that we are of worth, then we stand a good chance of programming our own children to receive the same message.

To take the computer analogy one stage further, it is possible to update the programmes in our computers. For some time I operated a wordprocessing package called *Works 3.0* but the person who trains us in YFC in the use of our computers recommended that I update to *Works 4.0*. 'It is a better programme altogether,' she said, 'and will improve your efficiency and range of options for very little cost.' She was right and the update has proved its value.

In the same way our self-confidence and self-worth can be updated and our brains reprogrammed and I hope this book will be part of that updating, that learning process.

I have looked at some principles expounded in a secular setting but I believe there are also some fundamental standards which are set out in the Bible. I make no excuses for using terms like 'fundamental standards' in an age when fundamentalism is regarded as almost the same as terrorism and standards are those which the individual sets for herself or himself. Even if you are not a believer in Biblical principles, I would ask you to glance through the next few pages, just to get a glimpse of what wisdom is available from the thousands of years over which the Bible was written.

Genesis 2:24 For this reason a man will leave his father and mother and be united to his wife, and they will become one flesh.

This verse is not solely about marriage, it is about the transition by which each person moves from being the child of one family to being an adult member of another. This transition, from dependent childhood to acceptance as an adult member of society, features in some form in every human culture.

Cultural change may stretch the period over which this transition takes place, but the fact of the transition remains in every culture. The Bible affirms it, and affirms the role of the parent in guiding the child.

> Deuteronomy 32:11 Like an eagle that stirs up its nest and hovers over its young, that spreads its wings to catch them and carries them on its pinions. The Lord alone led him.

This is a beautiful picture of the mother eagle who wants to teach her young to fly, knowing the fledglings are ready but still being there to ensure no harm comes to them. In the same way, parents need to be ready to launch their children, giving them, as Tony Campolo, the well-known American speaker and sociologist puts it, 'Roots and Wings'.

The psalmist speaks of the renewal, in each generation, of the knowledge of God:

> Psalm 78:2(b)–4 I will utter hidden things, things from of old – what we have heard and known, what our fathers have told us. We will not hide them from their children; we will tell the next generation the praiseworthy deeds of the Lord, His Power and the wonders He has done.

The Bible speaks clearly of a God who wants to be involved in the process of adolescence, who has an interest in investing in the adults who will emerge from this process.

> Proverbs 22:6 Train a child in the way that he should go, and when he is old he will not turn from it.

This is usually interpreted in the general sense, 'the way that he should go' being the Christian way, but it can also be read in a narrow sense, specific to the individual: 'train up each child in the way that this unique child should go . . .' God is committed to developing the individual to his or her full potential.

Then there is the fulcrum verse which ends the Old Testament and comes before the New Testament.

> Malachi 4:6 God will turn the hearts of the fathers to their children and the hearts of the children to their fathers; or else I will come and strike their land with a curse.

This has both a promise and a judgement. We in YFC long to see the time when the heart of God, which is for family unity, should be reflected in the hearts of parents and their children throughout this land of ours. But we also recognise the stern warning that family breakdown will have a devastating effect upon the land. We are already beginning to see the consequences of this in the work we do with young people.

Luke 2:52 describes just what goes into this transition, the transformation of a child into an adult, in Jesus' adolescent years. 'And Jesus grew in wisdom and stature, and in favour with God and men.' Adolescence is not a passive or neutral time, simply a waiting to become an adult, it is a time of growth and development, of preparing for adulthood.

The Bible speaks of God's total commitment to each new generation. This is seen in Colossians 3:20 where the apostle Paul tells children, 'Obey your parents in everything, for this pleases the Lord.' He then goes on to address parents, 'Fathers, do not embitter your children, or they will become discouraged.' We need to teach our children obedience so they learn to obey God the Father and as parents our duty is to encourage our children.

We believe that the Bible shows that God is:

a. Committed to the development of each unique adolescent into the adult he has called them to be.
b. Committed to the central role played by parents in this process.
c. Committed to the supportive role played by the extended family and wider community.

d. Realistic in understanding the stresses and tensions that change and growth can cause.
e. Generous in making available wisdom and strength to struggling parents.

Chapter 2

Initiation and the Teenager

In pre-industrial cultures, the transition from childhood to adulthood was accomplished in a short time span, and often accompanied by a decisive ceremony, such as the Jewish Bar Mitzvah.

Nelson Mandela describes in painful detail the day, at the age of sixteen, when he was accepted into adulthood in a traditional ceremony of circumcision. Each boy is trained to cry out, at the very moment of circumcision, 'Ndiyindoda!' which means, 'I am a man!'. The ceremony, over several days, takes place in an isolated place, where special lodges have been constructed to house the 26 young men being initiated at the same time. He writes:

> At the end of our seclusion, the lodges and all their contents were burned, destroying our last links to childhood, and a great ceremony was held to welcome us as men to society. Our families, friends, and local chiefs gathered for speeches, songs, and gift-giving.[2]

Western society has for the most part lost the remnants of such initiation rites, and has both extended and blurred the gap between childhood and adulthood. The phrase 'adolescent' was first coined in 1905 by G. Stanley Hall. By the 1950s the concept of the 'teenager' had arrived: a half-child, half-adult creature who hovers uncertainly between dependence and acceptance, and for whom the transition will last for anything from six years upwards. All the signs are that adolescence is getting longer, as children enter the phase earlier, and wait longer, by choice or default, to settle into stable relationships and fixed economic activity.

The following table is taken from Pete Gilbert's book, *Understanding Teenagers*. Pete is one of Britain's leading experts on teenagers, and was for many years with Youth for Christ.

AGES OF RESPONSIBILITY

10 years – responsible for criminal offences (It needs to be noted that currently the law as it stands at the time of writing, places the burden on the prosecution to show clearly that the child knew that what was done was seriously wrong as opposed to simply naughty. This is known as 'doli incapax'. However, under the Government's Crime and Disorder Bill currently going through Parliament, doli incapax will be removed.)

13 years – can be employed for light work

14 years – can go in a pub (but not buy alcohol)

15 years – can open a Giro account

16 years – can leave school
– can hold driving licence for a moped
– can work a 48-hour week
– can buy tobacco
– can buy wine and beer with meals
– can consent to medical treatment
– can get married with parental consent
– girls can consent to sexual intercourse
– can buy Lottery tickets

17 years – can go into betting shop (but not bet)
– can become street traders
– can hold ordinary driving licence

18 years – age of majority
– can get married without parental consent
– can drink alcohol in pubs
– can watch adult films

        – can place bets
        – can make legal contracts
        – can be sent to ordinary prison
        – can be tattooed
        – can vote
        – can consent to homosexual practices
21 years – can become an MP
        – can adopt a child

Gilbert writes, 'These produce a plethora of anomalies as the transfer of privilege and responsibility, with its attendant tensions and pressures in Western society, is not only gradual, but often unhelpful!'[3]

It seems fair to describe adolescence as an artificial extension of the initiation process: thus there is work to do in helping young people and parents through it, and in applying Biblical wisdom. The emotional needs of the child are the same as they might be were the initiation process condensed into a short ceremony. Adolescents stand caught between memories of the childhood they now know to be over and prospects of an adulthood in which they have not yet tested out their skills.

They need to know that they belong and are loved, and that the family who has nurtured them to date will still be there for them, not casting them out but helping them to move on. They need to know that there is a place for them in the adult society into which they are being initiated.

At the end of one parenting seminar a 19-year-old took issue with me for saying teenagers were not adults. She was angry and hurt and asked how dare I make such a statement when she felt strongly that she was in every way an adult. She challenged the concept being put forward that teenagers were still children. This prompted me to find a definition of an adult. Gordon R Lowe, who was a professor of psychology and psychiatry in Ontario, puts it like this:

> An adult is a person with a settled identity, a settled or an appropriate career, someone who has achieved a mature sexual identity and

integrated their own ethical standards with those of society. In other words, the adult's identity will be a stable one as long as the person knows who they are, where they stand, where they are going and (perhaps) who is going with them.[4]

So it can be argued that to be an adult there has to be a level of stability which is not always apparent in those who consider themselves adults and who the law declares have reached that state. However, for the purposes of this book I take the view that teenagers are passing through a transition period and have not yet arrived at adulthood.

To ensure the successful launch of teenagers into adulthood they need two essential types of 'rocket-fuel'. First of all they need parental nurturing that enables them to feel good about themselves and know they are loved. This is essential if they are to relate intimately to others. Secondly they need a store of completed but shorter journeys into independence on which to draw before the final launch takes place. These fuels are basic to all human emotional need and help to establish their identity which is fundamental to achieving adulthood.

Jane Gordon, a 38-year-old writer once wrote, 'It baffles me why no one has found a cure for adolescence. Today there is no hormonal complication that cannot be wiped out by a pill, a patch or a potion.' She goes on to ask in an article written for a national daily newspaper, 'Why can't you give a teenage daughter Hormone Extraction Therapy?'[5]

Now all of us recognise that adolescents are going through a period of rapid change but the truth is there is no way of avoiding the process. For some parents they wonder what all the fuss is about, whilst others struggle with their offspring through every day-by-day mood swing and exasperation. I want to help you through the changes and I believe there is a way to prepare for these years.

In 1979 the New York Marathon was won by Rosie Ruiz and she triumphed again in Boston the following year running in looking as fresh as the moment the race started. She received the congratulations of the waiting media scrum with all due modesty: she had after all won two very prestigious prizes in one of athletics' most demanding and self-examining races. However, one journalist wondered why he had not heard the name mentioned among the leaders during the race and began to make some enquiries. It soon became evident that Rosie had not run the full course. She had, in fact, joined the race with less than two kilometres to run and had slipped in unnoticed among the leaders and had romped home fresh and suitably happy to be awarded the prize.

Unfortunately there is no way to avoid this process of growing from child to adult through the teenage years. Indeed, many of the values and character traits which mark us out as individuals are determined in these years.

Let's look more closely at the process of change.

Chapter 3

Adolescence:
Change – the Roller-Coaster Ride

Commentators agree that adolescence can be broken down into key stages. Recognising that cultural change is bringing the actual starting-point of adolescence earlier, we have assumed a stage from 11–14, widely acknowledged to be the modern-day entry point into 'teenage years'. Our research indicates an overall lowering of the cultural thresholds of adolescence, so that in practice the issues faced by 16-year-olds in, say 1965, will be faced by 11- and 12-year-olds today. It is important for parents to recognise this and to be ready for the teenage years to start earlier than was their own experience.

We have identified three stages, equivalent approximately to 11–14, 15–17 and 18–21. Research indicates that these stages are distinguished by the different emphasis on dependency.

Stage 1   **Dependent but looking outward:**
           Discovery and experiment, from the relative safety
           of belonging.
Stage 2   **Inter-dependent – Changing feelings and attitudes:**
           Contact with the real world, contradictions of
           wanting both the freedom of independence and the
           security of belonging.
Stage 3   **Independence:**
           Consolidation, personal choice, growing
           responsibilities of independent adult life.

NB: It is important that these stages are not understood legalistically or rigidly. Different individuals, in different circumstances, will pass through these changes at different speeds, and sometimes unevenly. Boys and girls will tend to change and grow at an uneven pace, and individuals may be at stage 3 in one area of their lives but still hovering between 1 and 2 in another area.

If adolescence is anything, it is a process of change. Someone has said that change is inevitable, except from a vending machine. Adolescents are not machines, they are changing people in a changing world, and are often shaken and stirred by the changes they go through. Parents need to be prepared for change, to expect the unexpected, to make huge adaptations and accommodations; not so as to indulge the child but in order to offer the most supportive and healthy environment possible. Change will be apparent in the five areas of development in which the personality is formed. These will span all three stages of adolescence, with varying degrees of intensity. Remember that each young person is different, so you need to expect brothers and sisters to display characteristics which differ in time and intensity in comparison with their siblings.

Physical

This is a period of rapid physical growth with the result that adolescents are always tired, always hungry, always clumsy, always irritable. As they grow fast, so they eat a lot. Their emotions are worn out by physical change, so they become short-tempered and display a tendency to victimise siblings. It is helpful to know that all teenagers are awkward, not just yours. Their bodies are growing so fast their brains have not caught up and so they tend to knock things over and lose the control they had when younger. All in all, change equals stress!

It is at this time when the cry from parents is often heard, 'You clumsy oaf!' This is not helpful, except perhaps in relieving some tension. Try to think how your teenager is feeling. She may have enjoyed ballet for a number of years but has suddenly grown to the point where the movements are no longer second nature and are even painful; he may no longer be selected for the football team having always been good at sport and your personal attack may scar him for life. Some young women (and, more rarely, young men) get so anxious about their appearance they take drastic measures to try and change the way they look and may even fall prey to eating disorders. Your love and affirmation will help them through this time.

What your children need at this stage in their physical development is understanding. I suggest keeping a growth chart with dates and heights on, say, the door post to the kitchen. It will be a reminder how quickly they are growing and an opportunity to talk about the changes that are taking place.

Puberty

Part of the physical change which all adolescents face is puberty. We shall talk more about sexuality later but suffice it for now to understand that your child will experience waking hormones.

Ally Oliver, the editor of *Bliss* magazine writes that she considers children can never get enough sex education. According to an article published in *Report*, June/July 1997 (a magazine produced by the Association of Teachers and Lecturers), *Bliss* magazine was judged as irresponsible by the Teenage Magazine Arbitration Panel. In a defence of her position in the same *Report* article, Oliver writes,

> Yes, our readers will be tempted to buy the magazine because of a coverline on a sexual issue. That's because a rampantly hormonal 15-year-old is desperate to glean any information she can on a subject she is half-knowledgeable about and which dominates so much of her life. Sex education in schools is vital. But magazines are part of the social learning package too. Sex is relevant to our readers but so is fashion, love, family and friends; 95 per cent of the articles in *Bliss* deal with these other aspects of life.

All I can say is that it is a pity they do not appear to market the magazine on anything other than sex. I believe parents have an important role to play in guiding their children through the early months of puberty. Girls need to be told about the monthly menstrual cycle, before it arrives, in terms that are clear and unemotional. Boys need to be warned about wet dreams, the deepening voice and that it's common to get erections when you don't want them. Both girls and boys need to be told that their bodies are different from the opposite sex.

At this time adolescents become very self-conscious and start worrying about their appearance, often comparing themselves with other school acquaintances who are more or less mature physically than they are. As they change, so sexual experimentation begins, including masturbation, homosexual encounters of a minor scale and crushes on peers or adults. These can be times of intense fear of inadequacy for young people and positive, straightforward help and advice from unembarrassed parents is invaluable.

Mental

Someone has said that youth is wasted on the young. At a time when their mental capacity is still growing young people have so many life-changing decisions to make that they do not seem to have the time to enjoy the experience of being young. Erik Erikson, a child psychologist, has put forward the idea that adolescence is a staging post between being a child and an adult, a sort of inn where the horses are changed and the passengers wait for the next part of the journey. This fits well with our thoughts that this is a journey for both parents and children.

During the teenage years the young person moves from thinking in concrete to more abstract terms. It is interesting to undertake a discussion with a group of young people from a wide cross-section of ages, say from 13 to 18 years old. The younger members of the group will find it quite hard to talk in terms of feelings. They will answer the question, 'How do you feel?' with the rather childish retort, 'With my finger tips', whilst the older ones will be perfectly at ease in expressing their thoughts in more abstract terms.

But this does present challenges for the parent, especially the Christian parent. Well-worn arguments which to parents may seem really old hat, are new and exciting to the young. J. John, the well-known speaker and writer, tells of the time he was at a school and told the audience they may ask any questions: not a practice recommended for the inexperienced. A sixth-form student thought he would take J. John on and with plenty of nods and winks to his mates asked, 'Have you ever seen God then?' J. John's reply came quick as a flash, 'Have you ever seen Queen Victoria?' This drew some sniggers but eventually there was silence. 'You have never seen Queen Victoria because you lived at the wrong time. If you had lived in first-century Palestine you could have seen God because Jesus was alive then and he is God.'

As young people change they become more curious, begin to have fantasies, and display the trend towards a quick turnover of 'ideas of the week'. The education system drives them to learn by self-discovery which encourages experimentation. Whilst there is nothing particularly wrong with this it can lead to experimentation in areas which are not necessarily healthy. As the change goes on, adolescents may show signs of undervaluing the experiences of others, especially adults and they may look around for role models from within their own generation.

They can display an intellectual stubbornness, which can be exasperating and they can also be argumentative, apparently just for the sake of argument. Teenagers appear to have a very short attention span and use of the words 'boring' and 'sad' will be common. All adolescents, it seems, are the same in this area. They will adopt short-lived enthusiasms; they want to change the world but can't be bothered to get up in the morning. They can be so hard to please.

Social

This is a period of change socially. This is an area where the changes for adolescents today are very different from those their parents experienced. Certainly for school leavers in the 1960s there was little thought given to not being able to obtain employment. These were the years of Prime Minister Harold Macmillan's 'You've never had it so good.' In 1975, 60 per cent of 16-year-olds were in full-time employment, but by 1988 only 22 per cent of all 16-year-olds had obtained a full-time job. In the same period there was a 50 per cent increase in those going on to further education.

These social changes make it more difficult for parents to relate to the pressures children are under but understanding and encouragement from parents as their teenagers move towards independence and seek a career are vital. Tony Campolo told us that he feels parents need to give greater guidance to their children in choosing a career and not abdicate all responsibility to the Careers Adviser at school.

During the teenage years, young people want independence and show a desire for both freedom and support (sometimes both at once!), and this can be confusing for parents who sometimes are expected to adapt instantly, almost by telepathic insight. Socially, young people come under a great deal of pressure from peer relationships which become significant at this time. However it is encouraging to know that in a survey published in 1990, 81 per cent of young people aged 15 to 20 said that the family was the single most influential thing in their lives. Our own research indicates that parents are still the greatest influence over their teenagers. We will expand more on this subject in Chapter 4.

Another aspect in their social development is the very strong fear of rejection (from both adults and peers). Dr James Dobson, the founder of 'Focus on the Family' and author of many books, writes about the supersignificance and all-consuming importance that is given to physical attractiveness by our present culture. He calls it the Gold Coin of Human Worth. The drive for social acceptance means that anyone who missed the queue when good looks were being handed out, can sometimes feel rejection whether real or perceived. He goes on to talk of an imaginary date.

Helen Highschool, to be honest, is not very gorgeous, her shoulders are rounded and she seems to have trouble remembering to close her mouth when thinking (that seems to worry her folks a lot). She has pimples distributed at random over her forehead and chin.

She has never had a real date before but in spite of the risks, has agreed to a blind date which almost signalled the end of the world. Charming Charlie arrived expecting to meet the girl of his dreams. Helen was not what he had in mind. The next day Charlie recounted his feelings. 'Her braces stuck out further than her chest. She had so much bridgework in her mouth you had to pay a toll to kiss.'[6]

The rejection felt by Helen went so deep that she felt on trial to the whole human race. As parents we all know the beautiful young women who blossomed in their late teens in the classic ugly duckling-to-swan fashion, but it is so hard to convince an adolescent who is feeling rejected that beauty is in the eye of the beholder and that who you are is more important than what you look like. Our culture dictates otherwise. As parents you can give invaluable support and acceptance. We have all been found guilty in the courts of the not-so-good-looking and, especially for Christian parents, we need to remind our young people (as well as ourselves) that we are made in the image of God and he regards us as special and unique. But regardless of faith, we are all unique human beings with the capacity to love and be loved.

Parents should be aware of the statistics recently published by the Schools' Health Education Unit which showed six out of ten girls (i.e. 60 per cent) in their mid-teens thought they needed to lose weight, although only 15.3 per cent weighed too much for their age. Many young women are missing meals in order to lose weight and by doing so may be causing themselves psychological or physical harm. Deficiencies of iron and calcium in the diets of 14- and 15-year-old adolescents is giving concern to dietary experts. As parents you have a duty to your children to affirm them but also to give them a balanced diet. This can be difficult when so many teenage girls prefer to look like the really slim models on the front of glossy magazines. There is not the time or space to cover this subject in any great depth but if you are concerned about eating disorders do not hesitate to speak to your GP.

Dobson goes on to call intelligence the Silver Coin of Self-Worth. He writes, 'When the birth of a first-born child is imminent, his parents pray that he will be normal – that is "average". But from that moment on, average will not be good enough.'[7] Each of us can recall a moment in our own childhood when the blood rushed to our faces as we made some dreadful faux pas which everyone but us thought so side-splittingly funny. We felt the sting of ridicule and rejection. Every young person experiences uncomfortable moments like these but, alas, some youngsters live with disgrace every day of their lives.

As parents of teenagers going through the social changes in their lives, you need to sharpen your memories of the times you were hurt and embarrassed so you can help your children through their hurts in turn.

For women, says Dobson, beauty retains its number one position throughout life. The reason is because she knows the average man can see better than he can think. For men, intelligence is the personal attribute that is valued most and this is rooted in the opinions of the opposite sex, since women value intelligence over handsomeness in men.

These are times of extremes and reactions to teasing or put downs can be over sensitive. However, in the fast-changing patterns of conformity and loyalty, young people will search for tribes to belong to. So they will be fans of pop stars, footballers, film stars, soap opera actors and will want to adorn their bedrooms with posters of their favourites but that is not so different from how you as parents behaved!

As they search for heroes to worship, there will also be those anti-heroes, the people who seem to kick against society, to whom young people will give special honour. They will show enthusiasm for larger-than-life heroic images and have a romantic outlook on life, an idealism, and even a refusal to accept mundane realities. As the social changes occur, adolescents will also, almost deliberately, 'test' their parents' tastes.

Another confusing area for parents can be the times when your youngster wants to be in the spotlight, when only the day before she was saying how she simply died because everyone was looking at her. Part of the social change is the awakening self-consciousness.

There was a very clever advertisement a few years ago, for a feminine hygiene product. It showed a schoolgirl entering the classroom with a bubble above her head which read, 'Everyone knows it's my period', the implication being that if she only were to buy the product, she could remain unnoticed.

As parents you need to be aware of the times when your teenager needs to be included but not in the spotlight, noticed but invisible! Yes, they can be a real pain sometimes!

Emotional

During the teenage years your home may resemble a busy railway terminal with people coming and going all the time. Some come only once while others become part of the furniture. You will also note a change during the adolescent years from your child being part of a group to being one of a couple each of the opposite sex. There is no particular age at which these changes take place and each young person is, of course, different.

These are times of intense and fluctuating emotions. The daughter who tells her parents she has found the man of her dreams and intends to marry him, is just as likely to bring a different boy home a fortnight later and declare the other one, 'Sad!' You will need to know that your young person will often need to be left alone in public, however, we recommend that hugs do not stop at the onset of adolescence. Obviously you need to choose your times to show affection in this way but hugs are an excellent way to keep affection flowing.

There is a lovely story about a Romanian orphanage where the conditions were dreadful and the neglected children were slowly but surely dying. However, the over-stretched doctor noticed that on one ward the children were getting better. An investigation was started into the reasons for this change. Was it the nursing care that was making the difference? No, the same nurses were caring for many other wards as well as the one where improvement was seen. Was it the food, perhaps the lighting, the outlook, the way the sun caught this particular ward? None of these things was found to be unique to this ward. Yet, the children were getting better.

So the doctor decided to get up very early one morning to monitor the ward for 24 hours to observe whether there was a lesson to be learned. The first person to visit the ward that morning was the cleaning lady. She got on her hands and knees and washed the floor but as she got to the first cot she stopped, stood up, picked up the child and held it, cooing and ahing into the little face. After a while she put the child back, got on her hands and knees, went on washing till she got to the next cot. Here the same thing happened, she got up, picked up the child and held it, cooing and ahing into the little face. Then she got back down on her knees and washed the floor.

The doctor realised that this small act of holding the children and showing affection was making the difference for this was the only ward the woman cleaned. There is never a time in our lives when we do not need the flow of affection by physical touch.

At the same time, adolescents are tied into a changing body and their emotions are often at the mercy of hormonal upheaval. They may feel from time to time that nobody is in control! Here there is a need for personal space and sensitivity. Remember they are not yet adults and you will have to treat each moment as it comes. Sometimes they will want you to give lots of hugs, other times they will brush you away. Do try to be understanding.

One of our workers asked her youth group what advice they would like to give parents, expecting something profound and useful. 'Well, Wendy, tell them not to cut our toe nails too short. This really causes us grief!' It never ceases to amaze me what teenagers find important.

With the best of your intentions your teenager may still feel no one understands. Someone has said that every adolescent believes they are the first adolescent in history! This can lead to a sense they are meeting the challenge alone, and as the young person's fears are often poorly articulated, they can be misunderstood by adults who may feel their love is being rejected. This is not the case, but adolescents need to talk on their own terms and at a time they choose, which rarely coincides with a time convenient to parents.

Dr Ross Campbell, Associate Professor of Paediatrics and Psychiatry at Tennessee University, gives some helpful advice on how to recognise those times when your adolescent wants to talk. All parents will be able to identify those times if they look for the clues. He writes about the teenager who really wants to talk on a subject which they find threatening, so instead of getting straight down to the point, will ask a question quite out of character. The alert parent will pick this up. For example, if your adolescent never asks about how your day went but suddenly does so, this is a clue that a deeper conversation is being looked for.

Campbell puts it like this:

> Parents must be alert for such unsolicited and sometimes puzzling gestures, usually a hesitant teenager's way of asking for time and focused attention. He is 'feeling us out', testing us to see what kind of mood and frame of mind we're in – to see if it is safe to approach us on an issue about which he feels uncomfortable.[8]

He says that for his own children he got used to the words, 'Oh, by the way' being the code to pay particular attention.

As has already been indicated, adolescents have not achieved a settled identity and part of the emotional change they go through is establishing this identity. The question, 'Who am I?' can lead to crises. Pressure on all sides to be this or that creates confusion, inconsistency, discouragement, and even anger.

As parents you must recognise your own fallibility and if young people have not already grasped this truth, they certainly will during the adolescent years. This realisation may cause anxiety as they come to terms with it emotionally.

Spiritual

One of the changes that will happen during these years is spiritual. Our research has shown that young people are leaving the church at a rate which has hardly slowed since the start of the decade. It is also true to say that the largest majority of those leaving are between 11 and 14 years of age. YFC has addressed this issue by introducing Rock Solid Clubs which are aimed at this age group. We have produced three years of week-by-week material, together with leaders' guides and a residential training weekend at a price every church can afford. If you would like to know more, please contact us at Halesowen (the address is at the front of this book).

In the early adolescent years young people are into a 'joining' faith, they feel the need to belong to something significant, the need for interest and activity, whilst often being reluctant to go into too much intellectual depth. This is the period they are still willing to accept their parents' faith.

Older adolescents are more into searching. They need to ask wide-ranging and sometimes shocking questions, often used to seek a reaction. You must remember they are now moving from accepting your faith to looking for something acceptable to the group they happen to belong to at the time. This very strong group-awareness can cause problems for parents who may view it as losing their authority and influence. However, we believe in the need for 'controlled rebellion', for, as Tony Campolo says, at least they have something to rebel against!

At this age, young people are looking for adult mentors apart from parents. The youth group leader is taken into the confidence of the older teenager more readily than parents. Be ready for this and, at the same time, look for ways to keep the channels of communication open. One parent complained to me as the youth group leader, asking why I knew where his son was and how come I was aware that he was doing some valuable babysitting. Whereas all he had said to his father, in answer to the question, 'Where are you going?' was the monosyllabic, 'Out!'

Many adolescents will be searching for something which they consider works. Some will already have come to the conclusion that church is boring and irrelevant and it is at this time when the authenticity of the parents' faith is examined with equal intensity as the orthodoxy. In other words, they will be looking to see whether you put your faith into action. Questions will come at you thick and fast.

'Why do you drink and smoke yourselves to death and try to tell me about drugs?'

'Why do you go on about me not getting into trouble with the law, when you always drive over the speed limit?'

'How can you go on about me not nicking stuff, when you're always on the phone to Dad from work?'

These are just examples of the type of examination your faith will be put under. And we haven't even started on the ones about what the Bible says on subjects of healing, selling all you have to give to the poor and loving your neighbour as yourself. They will be asking themselves whether it make sense and if it works for their parents. It is still true to say that Christianity is caught rather than taught. Your children need to see your faith in action; you are still their best role models in the faith.

We want our children as they become young adults to move into an 'owned' faith, one that is not second but first generation. We want them to be making personal choices, moving from 'group awareness' to a smaller number of more deeply valued relationships. At this time the church should be looking to allow them to be involved in ministry and leadership tasks, and as parents, you can be encouraging your newly emerging adult into these areas.

At this point you may well be asking what to do if your teenager declares they are no longer coming to church with you. I cover this subject in more detail in Chapter 9.

We have spent some time on the subject of change because we feel that an understanding of the process of adolescence can be a real help to parents as you cope with the mood swings, the questions and the highlights of the teenage years.

Chapter 4

Roots and Wings

One currently popular and very helpful analysis of parenting, describes the role of parents as being to provide their children with Roots and Wings. As Tony Campolo explains in an interview given to YFC in 1995:

> Roots. The Parents must communicate to the child a sense of stability and security: a sense of belonging, a sense of identity: a frame of family reference, so that who I am is firmly established and what our family stands for is firmly defined. The family must also provide Wings. That is, it must create within children a sense of imagination. The Bible says that when they no longer dream dreams or have visions, they perish. It is so important that parents get children to dream dreams; help them to imagine what they could be; help them to conceptualise in their imagination what the future might be if God has his way with them. To dream dreams, to help a child believe in himself.[9]

Parents preparing to face the journey of adolescence would do well to look into these twin ideas and analyse the extent to which their parenting to date has given to their children roots and wings. Then in the light of that examination plan ways in which they can do so.

Claire Short, who is a counsellor/therapist with her own clinical counselling practice, writes: 'So often obsessive protection is confused with love. It isn't. It can be a totally selfish act by parents, stunting their children's emotional development and preventing them from coping in today's society.'[10] As parents you need to be aware of the dangers of overprotection. Picking up kids at the school and taking them everywhere may, say some psychologists, breed a generation which grows up feeling it is perilous to be independent; without confidence in their own competence they will lack self-esteem and the skills to survive and raise a family.

During the teenage years your children will be looking for greater and greater independence and your main task is to establish their competence and readiness for the world of adulthood. The security of home is vital during these developing years and, in my experience, this need for security does not stop when the young person leaves home. It is helpful to remember that your teenager's readiness for independence is a sign of your success as parents.

Recent research indicates that the parents are still the strongest influence on their adolescent children – despite all the increases in pressure from peers and the media. These secondary influences often shape decisions at a transitory and superficial level, the fashions of the moment, but the long-term development of character, personality and values flows primarily from parents.

In a publication by the Family Policy Studies Centre called *Fathers and Fatherhood in Britain*, published in 1997, it was found that between 1 in 6, and 1 in 7 fathers live apart from some or all of their dependent children. The book goes on to say that this statistic can obscure the reality that 85 per cent of all fathers continue to live with all of their dependent children. But it is the changing role of fathers which has yet to be fully understood. There are calls for fathers to be more involved in their children's lives, to have close, caring and emotionally involved relationships with them. In the past, the term 'breadwinner' summed up the father's role but what comprises 'new' fatherhood is less certain.

In the book mentioned above, a group of 14-year-olds were asked about fathers. They appear to endorse the view that earning money was the most important activity for fathers, followed by giving care and love and being involved in domestic duties.

Seventy per cent agreed with the statement 'Children need a father to be as closely involved in their upbringing as their mother'. This should make us as parents review our roles and see how we can be involved with our adolescents in nurturing and caring for them, as well as bringing home the money.

In some extensive research carried out by YFC Associate Colin Piper, who is Director of South West Youth Ministries, he asked young people, 'What do you most appreciate about your mum and dad?' Those questioned admitted that they found it really difficult to articulate to their parents the things they really appreciated about them and you may not realise that your own children may say they would die rather than tell you these things themselves.

Piper lists six things that, once the young people had warmed to their theme, they said they appreciated about their parents:

1) Time and interest

Again and again it was time and interest that they appreciated and it was often what as parents you may feel is quite insignificant. But by showing your teenager that, even in a busy schedule, you have time for them is really important. However, it is equally important to realise that sometimes they will not welcome your time and interest and part of the skill of parenthood is to recognise when you need to back off.

I know of a family who are all mad keen on cricket. Both parents hold very responsible positions and the father is often abroad or away on business. Their sons really appreciate the fact that mum and dad take them to watch 'Day-Night' one-day cricket matches at Edgbaston, starting in the afternoon and finishing after dark under floodlights.

I can remember in my own case the time when both of my sons were becoming more fashion conscious and came to me one day and said that, quite frankly, I was an embarrassment to them by the way I dressed. Having lifted my jaw off the floor, I asked them what I should do about this. They both agreed to take me shopping. Marks and Spencers was definitely banned. Instead we went to 'Cromwell's Madhouse' and I was kitted out in less embarrassing attire. Of course, part of their thinking was that if they got dad in a good mood, when they spotted gear they really liked, it was not beyond the bounds of possibility that he would buy what they wanted as well. It worked every time.

Going shopping or going to a cricket match together may seem simple but adolescents have all said these sort of things help them to feel their parents have time for them and therefore they will have time for their parents when it comes to who influences their behaviour.

If you want to influence the young people in your family, it takes not only time but activity as well. Sharing your interests, doing things together helps build the relationships with your adolescents. Colin Piper tells of the young woman who burst into tears when she told him how she wished her parents had given her time and developed interests with her. Another girl told how she tried to spend time with her parents but all they wanted to do was watch television. She tried writing her letters in the same room, just to be with them and have something to do, but she got bored and then gave up!

Only recently, my older son, James, recalled the time he helped me with some do-it-yourself activity. It was the occasion when the cold-water tank in the loft needed replacement. I reckoned it would be a fairly straightforward job and decided to involve James in the planning and the execution. Now, I don't know about you but if anything is going to bring out the worst in me, it's D-I-Y. Val has banned me from ever, ever, papering a ceiling since the one occasion I tried and stormed out of the room leaving her with 5 metres of paper wrapped round her head! So to include James in this exercise was a real act of faith – on his part. I'm pleased to tell you we achieved the task but not before James had been left with his thumb over the end of a pipe to stop water leaking out, like the little Dutch boy who stuck his finger in the dyke, while I calmed down and decided how to get us out of the mess! And he still recalls the occasion with deep affection.

2) Approachability

The adolescents questioned talked about talking: why they find it hard to talk but how often, despite everything, they wished they could. They gave some clues as to what would make it easier to talk more, first on a chit-chat level but then more deeply. If the advertisements for BT are to be believed, fathers find it harder to talk than mothers. Before I get accused of making sexist comments, most of the young people we have talked to say they find it easier to talk to mum rather than dad. 'I'm more like dad but I'm closer to mum' is a common sentiment.

This is not surprising because men find it hard to switch on the emotional radar. We have been taught to cope and that it is a virtue to be the strong silent type. It is even more difficult for men who have positions of authority, or are involved in professions such as nursing, medicine, police, the church, where they have to remain emotionally detached at work. How do such people turn on the emotions when they walk through the front door?

The challenge is to be approachable and this means you will invariably need to take the initiative. If you have more than one child you will certainly find that they are all different. With our sons, one of them would chatter away, still does, whilst we would never have found out anything from the other one without asking lots of questions. One of the things we appreciate about them is their differences but it's so important to treat them as individuals if you want to retain that influence.

3) Understanding, reasonableness and protection

There is a tension between trust and restriction. As Piper puts it, 'Get it right and they go out confident and secure, get it wrong and they become bitter or vulnerable'. The young people he questioned spoke of reasoning and reasonableness as vital components in getting it right. You may feel that as a parent you need all the skill of a union negotiator trying to strike a deal with Rupert

Murdoch, but there are ways to develop these virtues that young people feel are so important.

It is clear from what young people themselves say that trust is an important element which will demonstrate parents' understanding. 'My parents trust us and because they do we're trustworthy and more responsible', said one 15-year-old. Perhaps surprisingly, those questioned were critical of parents who were, as they put it, a soft touch. It made them feel insecure. Young people know they are not yet able to fend for themselves and still want parents who are there to care and watch over them. Demonstrate you care and that you trust them and your influence will have long-lasting effects.

4) Affection and affirmation

Once more what young people are prepared to admit to a youth worker compared with what they communicate to their parents seemed to differ widely. One young woman put it like this, 'I appreciate my parents love me. They give me hugs, cuddles and kisses and I'm glad they do. From 15 to 17 I found it difficult to cuddle dad but he was usually sensitive . . . Love is less expressed verbally. They express pride verbally but rarely love.'

One of the young people in our church youth group told us how she was really pleased her dad had been to one of our seminars as he was now hugging her again and this made her feel loved and appreciated. But it seems clear that boys find it hard if their father suddenly starts to hug them after a long period of 'abstinence'. So the point is that affection and affirmation should continue to flow from childhood into adolescence and on into adulthood.

At this point I have to admit personally how hard I have found it to say, 'I love you' to my sons. I have tried to analyse this reticence. I have no problem in telling my wife that I love her, so is it a male to male thing? Would I have the same difficulty if I had a daughter? That is something I shall never know, even though I admit to having a daughter-in-law. I think it stems from my own upbringing. Hard as I try, I simply cannot recall my parents ever telling me they loved me but I never doubted it.

The very last action of my mother before she died demonstrated clearly to me her love and I shall never forget it. She was in hospital and fading away from us. She had fallen and broken her hip and the shock seemed to be too great for her. We were allowed to visit but only two of us were permitted by her bedside at any one time. I talked to her but there was not a flicker of recognition. It was painful but I had read that, even in the unconscious state, a person does hear what is said. I took her hand from under the bedclothes and stroking it, told her I loved her very much. The time came for us to allow other members of the family to see her and I left her bedside.

We all waited together in a room off the ward and when visiting was nearly over, we went to say our farewells. I said who I was and again not a flicker but this time she lifted her hand towards me; it was one of the most beautiful things she ever did for me.

It may be difficult to express our love to our children but by doing so, we retain an influence which will live for ever. For as the Bible puts it, 'love never fails'.

5) Encouragement and approval of who they are

Some of the young people questioned spoke of their real pain of being expected to live up to standards they could not achieve or being expected to become people they just could not be. Most though spoke of needing encouraging or even pushing. First and foremost they wanted inspiring to dream their own dreams and then encouragement to achieve them.

I cover 'Formulating Vision' in Chapter 13, using the interview with Tony Campolo, but it is important as we look at the influence parents have on their children, not to overlook the real damage that can be caused by great expectations. Many of the adolescents interviewed by Piper agreed that their parents pushed them too hard and then became angry when their children failed to live up to the demands placed on them.

By now you may be wondering how you can possibly get all these things right. The truth is none of us does, but the wonder of it all is that so many of our children turn out all right in the end. It is so important for you to realise that if things do go wrong, you must not feel condemned by your apparent failings. In the end, your children will make their own choices and it is they who must live with the consequences. For your part, you can still go on showing unconditional love. Whether Christian or not, this is your calling as a parent.

What we have been discussing in this section can really be summed up in to one word: Communication. If you have been communicating with your children from the very day they were born and have not stopped simply because the responses became monosyllabic when the teenage years were reached, then there is a good chance you can go on with the business of talking to each other.

The greatest thing you can do is inspire them to dream, encourage them to think who they might be. In a culture which values too highly the things people do, I believe it's much more important to get your children to dream of who they might be. Although I know some readers will criticise me for writing this, I take the greatest pride when people tell me, 'What really nice young men your sons have turned out to be'.

6) Understanding of the world

As parents you need to know that your adolescent children still feel insecure in the world. Piper found that this was even more so when parents seemed unable to relate to the world their teenagers were having to face day by day, let alone help them in it. One 14-year-old girl said, 'The perfect parent is the one who understands the world I'm growing up in.'

One of my objectives in writing this is for parents to have a better understanding of the world of the adolescent enabling them to see things from the young person's point of view. We shall look at their world in more detail later on. It is helpful to understand that young people do appreciate that experience of the wider world counts for a lot and this their parents have got, whilst they are still acquiring the necessary knowledge. When this understanding is translated into regular communication, rather than confrontation, young people appreciate their parents so much more.

However, you should not be surprised when your children look elsewhere for advice. This is not to say they do not value your influence but, as one young person put it, 'I talk to my friends more than my parents because their experience is different'. Val and I were initially concerned that our sons seemed to be discussing more intimate things with our lodger who was studying at the time at Spurgeon's College. But we came to realise that they were seeking a different point of view from someone who could be more objective. We could get a bit emotional and not very practical on occasions.

When I talked about this with James and Andy as part of our discussions for this book, they took a very positive line. Both said how much they valued, as teenagers, being allowed into our world and into our friendships. We never had friends who were referred to as 'Auntie' Nikki or 'Uncle' Simon, as some of our friends referred to Val and me but, as James and Andy reminded me, if they were our friends they were theirs as well. As a result, it was a natural step for them to talk to these friends about the problems they were facing. Both James and Andy wanted me to advocate the inclusion of your adolescents in your circle of friends and even encourage them to seek advice and a different perspective on things from that which you, as parents, hold on a particular issue. It builds trust between you, your friends and your children.

One girl told Piper her parents would tell her, 'Well you know God loves you.' She went on, 'That may be true but it isn't that much help being told it.'

Colin Piper comments, 'Thinking about it I cannot recall Jesus telling anyone: "Never mind at least God loves you." He always seemed to get involved practically.'

If we as parents show we have time for our children, if we make home secure, open and fun, then our children, as they grow through adolescence, are less likely to look elsewhere for their values and influences. Look elsewhere they inevitably will, and we'll consider this later, but if you want to remain the strongest influence on your children, do not expect it to just happen. It won't. Like all good parenting, it takes time, effort and forethought.

Chapter 5

You Are On a Journey Too

The last, important element in knowing the landscape is recognising that you, too, are part of it. Often the greatest turbulence will be found where two rivers meet. In Exmoor there is a beauty spot called Tarr Steps where an ancient footbridge crosses the River Lyn. The stones of this bridge are enormous, over two metres in length and obviously weighing hundreds of kilograms. In August 1952 there was a freak storm which caused major flooding in Lynton and Lynmouth, destroying property in the towns and claiming the lives of 34 people. At Tarr Steps, two rivers meet at ninety degrees and such was the turbulence caused by the water that the stones were picked up and taken downstream many hundreds of metres.

You need to know that your adolescent is not the only one experiencing change: you, too, are on a journey of growth, development and change.

Psychotherapists explain that when asked to treat children and teenagers, they customarily refer to them in medical notes not as 'the patient' but as 'the identified patient'. Their point is that young people in difficulty are often identified as the source of the problem, the ones in need of treatment, but that, in reality, the problem lies equally with the family, school, society or parents. What is true in the minority of serious cases which are referred to professional counsellors is also true, in a more general sense, for all of us. Our children do not travel alone – we are with them, and caught up, often, in our own turbulence of change and adaptation.

There are five factors which will be a feature of your journey as a parent of teenagers. The first is simply the fact that you are reaching the mid-point in your lives. A fact many of us want to try and forget! You as parents are probably hitting middle age just as your children are hitting adolescence. As someone said, 'You know you've reached middle age when all you exercise is caution'. Your own crisis of identity and self-worth is compounded by the fact that your children choose this moment to start questioning and challenging you.

The second factor to bear in mind is pressure. The adolescent years also often coincide with the years in which the most demands are made on parents in terms of careers. It is at this time when you have reached the pinnacle of your career and all the pressures this entails, including long hours of work, that your children will be going through the teenage years. Unfortunately, it is also true to say that there are those parents who, rather than working longer hours, find themselves the victims of 'downsizing' the euphemism for redundancy. This brings its own pressures.

For the person in this predicament, the loss of self-esteem can be devastating at a time when the young people in the home will be needing theirs built up. It is not unusual for a person being made redundant to feel they are on the scrap heap and it is not unusual for parents and children to experience the inability to secure a job at the same time. Such pressures are very real and often unavoidable.

As the family has grown up and you have decided to have no more children, moves are often made to a house large enough for all the family to have their own space. You will have mortgaged to the highest level possible as this is the last move you intend to make. You are now fully extended financially. This brings its own pressure, especially when interest rates rise and tax relief falls. Of course, as I have said, there is another side to this coin. The person who has been made redundant, or whose career is not progressing, may have to consider moving in the opposite direction, to a smaller house, to reduce overheads. The pressure this brings is enormous. Teenagers can be insensitive at times like these, only seeing things from their point of view. Having to share a bedroom again because of financial constraints, may trigger all sorts of conflicts.

Good preparation needs to include strategies to fight off this pressure at times when you know that your own children will be struggling.

The third factor relates to relationships. Marriages for many reasons, including mid-life crisis and pressure, can often be under strain just as children enter adolescence and your frustrations can easily be projected onto the wrong people. Some of us enter marriage with rose-coloured spectacles and when the children come along problems may follow.

Steve Gaukroger, senior minister at Gold Hill Baptist Church and a well-known Spring Harvest speaker, talks of the rose-coloured view of marriage which some people hold. He says people think he and his wife Jan are up at 5.30 a.m., they spend two hours on their knees in Bible study and prayer and at 7.30 a.m. their eldest daughter knocks on the door and says, 'Daddy, I've finished my Bible Study notes, can I borrow a commentary from your study so I can get more into God's word? And by the way, I've laid breakfast.'

The family all sit down together for breakfast and their seven year-old asks, 'Mummy, how long did Jehoshaphat reign in Judah?'

At 8.45 a.m. the children skip happily off to school and Steve goes on his visits and when he returns at 6 p.m. there is a smell of fresh baking pervading the house and after the meal, the children run up to their rooms to do their homework. Jan and he sit comfortably on the settee, have a romantic evening together and are in bed by 10 p.m.

We all are aware of the opposite extreme. We have to shout at the kids to get up every morning, tapping that part of the anatomy which is necessary to get them moving. Breakfast is eaten on the run and the family all dash off to their places of work and education. At 11.30 p.m. at night we fall exhausted into bed. He says to her, 'Darling, shall we make love?' She replies wearily, 'Why?' To which he says, 'For old-time's sake!'

Another pressure which you may come under at this time relates to ageing parents. Often, just as our children are reaching adolescence, so our parents are needing more of our time, more of our care and more of our patience! People have shared with us as we have done parenting seminars of the real pressure they have been under from elderly parents, especially when they do not live in the same locality.

It is often at the time when your children are struggling with the pressure of adolescence that your own memories of your teenage years can be triggered and they can be very painful. The effect upon your memory is the fourth factor to consider on your journey. Parents have often buried the struggles they themselves went through as teenagers, until their own children provoke the emotions. Areas of behaviour in which you find yourself most frustrated and angered by your teenager may reflect the area in which you most struggled. Part of your preparation should include the realisation that your memories can become reality all over again in the behaviour and characteristics of your teenager.

Finally there is the question of codependency. Much is made of the child's journey from dependence to independence, but parents, too, can be dependent on their children. You often need to be needed, and your own sense of identity and self-worth can be built on your children's need of you. Adolescence takes not only them, but you, on the road to independence!

For all these reasons, accompanying children through adolescence can be a healing and enriching experience. Parent-child conflict, which we talk about in more detail later, when rightly handled, may lead to healthy changes for both. Families which hold together through these stresses and strains will often emerge deeply bonded, with relationships that will go on to withstand every attack. You may be frightened of losing the child whose very dependence on you reinforces your self-worth but you have the prospect, as you lose that child, of gaining a friend for life!

* * * * *

As I come to the end of the first stage in the journey, I want to make some suggestions for reflection and action. Not all these suggestions will be appropriate to every situation: they are here primarily to stimulate your own thinking about appropriate preparation. Most apply equally to a lone parent or to a couple, depending on your situation. (We shall be including some additional material for lone parents at the end of the book.)

Reflection

- Take some time out to remember your own adolescent years. What were your struggles? How did you feel about your parents' attitudes to you? If you still have diaries or letters from that time, take another look at them. Prepare to help your child by re-familiarising yourself with the whole context of adolescence.

- If your parents are still alive, talk to them about your own growth through adolescence. Think through your own situation as you approach this journey: what are the pressures and struggles you face which might be made worse by potential adult-child conflict? What can you do, in advance, to reduce these?

- Where you have specific concerns or fears about your own capacity to survive the turbulence of the teenage years, find a minister or counsellor with whom you can be honest, and ask for advice and/or prayer.

- Think through the years of your child's life to date, and be prepared to put right any wrongs you have done. If you have been unduly critical, short-tempered, harsh or judgemental, be ready to clear the air as they turn ten or eleven. Admit to them your weaknesses.

Communication

- Talk as a couple (or with other supporting adults) about the years that lie ahead. Discuss together what might be difficult, and what you might be able to do in advance.

- Ask a friend who knows both you and your child(ren) well to be honest with you about the strengths and weakness in your relationships. What is there in your behaviour which is likely to be inflammatory in a parent-child conflict? Establish the same honesty as a couple.
- Talk to your pre-adolescent about some of the changes that are coming. Use their tenth birthday as the hook on which to hang a one-adult-to-one-child evening out to talk together. Buy them a preparing-for-puberty book and give it to them, with the promise that you are happy to talk through anything in it that they don't understand.
- Consider creating a 'Family Council' to discuss areas such as behaviour, discipline, family choices and life together.
- Identify people around you whom you would trust to be observers and supporters of your family through these years – perhaps someone whose children have now grown up. Agree with them that they will have opportunities to be honest with you as these years progress.
- Talk to the youth leaders in your church, making sure that they know that you trust them, and are prepared to encourage your child to do so.

Culture

- Become an observer of youth culture. Read a few magazines, buy a few tapes or CDs, watch *Top of the Pops*, listen to the radio. Start watching a TV show of your child's choice, with them, once a week, and make it a regular date. Look and listen so as to learn, not to judge.
- Get involved with other parents to discuss cultural issues: learn where the real dangers lie and where it is just a question of taste.
- Make some notes, in advance, of cultural boundaries you feel to be fair: issues in which you will establish a rule and stick to it. Decide in advance at what age you will allow certain key freedoms.

- Encourage your child to invite friends to spend time at your home. Learn their first names and try to retain them! Get into the habit of obtaining the names and phone numbers of the parents of your children's friends.

Action

- Ask each person you meet who has grown-up children for two suggestions of things they did right and two warnings of things they would do differently given their time again.
- Make plans for privileges which you are going to give to your children when they become teenagers: the right to an adult-level vote in family decision making, the right to insist you knock before entering their room, the right to eat with you from time to time when you have an adult dinner party etc. Small privileges will serve as symbolic recognition that they are leaving childhood behind.

Conclusion to Stage 1: Knowing the Landscape

Key Points

ADOLESCENCE IS:

- A stage in the Biblical pattern of growth – dependent on parents, making the choice to leave, established in adult society.
- An extension of the cultural process of initiation, ending childhood and welcoming a 'new-born' adult.
- A time of change: physically, socially, mentally, emotionally and spiritually.
- A time when both child and adult are on a journey together.
- An opportunity for parents to provide roots and wings at an important stage in their child's life.

Stage 2

Planning the Route

Chapter 6

Culture

Having taken a look, in broad terms, at the journey of adolescence, I now want you to focus on how you can plot your way through it. This will include identifying some of the landmarks of the journey, suggesting values that will be of help to you along the way and making proposals of practical ideas that others have found beneficial.

These are some of the key areas which you will have to deal with as you accompany children through adolescence, and for which you can begin preparing well in advance.

The extension of adolescence and its recognition as a separate age group has been much accentuated by the development of global teenage culture. The Lausanne Commission for World Evangelisation published a report in 1978 which defined culture as:

> An integrated system of beliefs, values, customs and institutions which bind a society together and give it a sense of identity, security and continuity.

Teenage culture began in the 1950s with the first experiments in pop music, but has now extended into a huge multi-billion dollar industry spanning the globe, employing thousands and accounting for millions of hours of television and radio time. A full exploration of the depths and significance of youth culture would take more than a whole book of its own, but it may be helpful to quote from Michael Gallagher SJ, teacher of theology at the Gregorian University in Rome, and minister in the field of Faith and Culture in Ireland. His book contains a number of metaphors to describe culture. He writes that culture is like:

• an ocean, surrounding us as water a fish
• an environment that seems natural, especially if it is the only one we know
• the air we breathe, that may be healthy or polluted
• a lens, something we see through without realising that it is not the only way of seeing
• a filter, allowing through certain images of normality but not others
• a set of blinkers, censoring what can be seen
• an iceberg of the common sense of a group, which stays largely submerged or unconscious
• a baby's building bricks, the basis for creating a world
• a conspiracy of silence, imposed by the past
• a playground of possibilities, inviting one to creative freedom
• an ever-present horizon, beyond which one cannot see.[11]

For the purposes of effective parenting, we offer six observations about culture.

You are not the only influence on your child!

Like it or not, youth culture plays a huge role in shaping the minds of young people. Parents will increasingly need to deal with voices competing for the attention of their children and may increasingly find themselves negotiating, rather than dictating, their children's values.

In a paper published by the Family Policy Studies Centre it was discovered that fathers spend on average four minutes each day with their children; mothers do a little better at seven minutes. One father was bemoaning to Tony Campolo the fact that he did not know where his son got his values from. Asked how long he spent each day with the boy, he replied that it was about four minutes. In answer to the question as to how long his son spent watching television, he said it was about four hours. And he wondered where his son got his values?

The pressure is rising!

It was the Duchess of York who is reported to have said that if you're tired of shopping, you're going to the wrong shops! We now live in a 'shop till you drop' culture in which shopping has become the number one Sunday activity. Popular culture has become history's greatest money-making industry, exporting its products worldwide and backing its sales with unprecedented promotional pressure. Your children may be dealing with 'pressure to buy' which far outstrips anything you were subjected to at their age.

Colin Morris, former Head of Religious Broadcasting at the BBC, says of one particularly powerful medium, 'Television's influence is all-pervasive. It is not simply a device like a vacuum cleaner which serves us: it is an environment that wraps us round like a blanket.'

Culture is neither all bad nor all good

Judging all youth culture as bad and attempting to shut it out from the family home is naïve, probably impossible and ultimately unhelpful. But letting it flood in unchallenged is equally dangerous. Rules, boundaries and wisdom will all be needed in handling the influence of popular culture, particularly as the 'information highway' opens up. It is important to know that it is possible to ask your Internet provider to screen out material which you do not want to receive from the World Wide Web.

It is safer to learn to swim than to spend your life avoiding water!

A story is told of a group of parents whose houses backed on to a reservoir. They pleaded with the local council to build a fence to prevent their children getting near the water. They sent petitions to the water company to try to persuade them to fence the reservoir perimeter. All without success. So, they got together and taught their children to swim.

It really is no good saying that we will not go into the pool until we have learned to swim. Popular culture is a deep lake of information and entertainment. Young people can play safely and happily in it, but they can also drown. Your ultimate responsibility is to teach your child to swim – to make wise, informed critical choices.

Youth culture is often backed by peer pressure

As has already been mentioned, young people are highly driven by the need to belong; peer acceptance is at the top of their motivational agenda. In the modern world, this acceptance is often mediated through shared cultural icons: fashion, music, celebrities. What appears on the surface to be a simple matter of personal taste and cultural choice, is in fact driven by strong forces of peer pressure. You need to know that the cry, 'Everyone has seen the video', is invariably not true!

I have heard of schoolgirls being bullied because they wear the wrong kind of 'Kickers'. The drive to wear the right designer gear is very strong and parents often ask us how to negotiate this difficult area. There is no easy solution. One exasperated parent demanded, 'How do you teach your child the value of money?'

We believe that preparation is essential. Before they have reached their teenage years you should do all you can to teach them about money. Trust them with an allowance but as they get older, expect them to buy more of their own things out of the allowance as it increases in monetary value. Perhaps some statistics may help at this point.

Young people aged between 13 and 18 spend an average of £8.40 a week on everything from fast food to designer clothes. Today's brand-conscious young are handling far more cash than you as parents ever did in your youth. Fifteen year-olds spend, on average, a little less than £17 a week.

Around 759,000 children aged between 11 and 15 earn money doing household chores, babysitting, working in shops and delivering newspapers. Some 40 per cent hold down a regular job.

The Times of Saturday, 22 August 1998, reported these facts and went on to mention a 13-year-old girl who supplements her pocket money by occasionally working in a shop. She spends her £2 a week pocket money on magazines and chocolate but the £3 an hour she earns at the shop she is using to decorate her room.

Many young people adopt a similar attitude to this teenager. Her parents give an allowance which they consider sufficient but it is supplemented so that the young person can buy and do much more of what she wants.

Our son was at university when he came to a seminar to support us. During question time this topic came up and, rather unfairly, I asked him to explain how we as a family handled the situation from his point of view. He reminded us that we agreed as parents the amount we were willing to pay for trainers and such like, and if this was not sufficient to purchase the ones he wanted, he would save his own money until he had enough to go and buy them. This, he reckoned was fair enough and the principle applied to all the designer gear he wanted.

I would go further and advise you that it is not wise to try and prevent your teenager from wearing designer clothing. I do know of some parents, especially Christian ones, who consider that the whole designer clothes business panders to the culture in which we live and they insist that their children be different. Whilst I have every sympathy with this attitude and would want to applaud adults who do not purchase such clothes for themselves, I do want to strike a note of warning to you as parents on behalf of teenagers.

As I have already said, I know of girls who were bullied for wearing the wrong 'Kickers'. I would, therefore, advocate a balanced approach if at all possible, for two reasons. Firstly, consider the ridicule which your daughter or son may face at school. Some teenagers may appear to cope with this, but it can be terrible for others who become the butt of jokes and snide comments. Secondly, your action may make too much of the issue which could lead to your child wanting and, eventually, buying even more designer clothes, to make up for the deprivation they felt as a teenager. In the end, you will have to decide where to strike the balance.

Another YFC worker told me of the family he knew who used the Child Benefit to help their children budget. Apparently, when their children reached the age of 13 they handed over the Child Benefit in full to the teenagers who were then expected to purchase all their school equipment and uniform, together with all the other clothes they wished to buy. This seems to be working well and is empowering the young people themselves who say they are satisfied with this approach.

These examples are, of course, from middle-class backgrounds and I know of families who have to use the Child Benefit to pay for other essentials such as food. However, the two ideas have certain principles which can be adapted to suit your particular situation.

In talking to teachers, however, a different opinion emerges. There is a real concern that the drive to earn money in children's spare time will have an adverse effect upon their education. Because of the physical changes teenagers are experiencing, part-time employment will make them tired and could well impinge upon time for homework. As always, a balance can be struck and I feel that it is important that you as a parent discuss the possibilities with your adolescents before they take a job and review the situation regularly to ensure it is not having an adverse effect.

Both my sons had jobs and I believe it had a positive effect on their handling of money. I also believe it helped them to get their homework out of the way without procrastination – except for watching the obligatory Australian soap operas.

Tastes do change

Human beings, by definition, value the things that they like and undervalue the things that they don't like. For example many of you reading these notes will not agree that 'The Who' are the greatest rock band ever. All too often the rejection of a new cultural form (rock music, rap, rave, this year's new fashion), is an expression not of eternal values but of taste. For Christian families, faith which does not relate to the cultural forms of the present will be deemed 'a thing of the past' and rejected.

So you should try and help your children to value those things which do not change or are a matter of taste such as friendship, truth, loyalty, morality. And remember, if you're being driven mad by the music thumping away in the bedroom just ask what it is they're playing as you really like it and want to play it yourself. They'll never play it again!

It is crucial to be aware of the extent to which you will encounter change as you take this journey. We have already looked at some of the internal changes that an adolescent goes through, and indicated that you yourself may well experience change at this time. You must also be clear that the very environment in which the journey takes place is changing. Young people do grow up under more pressure today than ever before and are faced with issues you as parents did not have to deal with in quite the same way. It is impossible for every family to adapt to every area of change but there are times when an understanding of the forces of social change can greatly aid communication. Our research indicates a number of areas in which change is currently dominating young lives.

Principal among these are:

Future Shock

This is the term Alvin Toffler coined as long ago as 1970[12] to describe our inability to deal with accelerated cultural change. Toffler was the first to see that it was the pace of social change, as well as its extent, that affected people. He writes about 'Personal

Security Zones'. These are places which are similar and predict-
able in an ever-changing world, for example McDonald's, which
remains the same whether it is Budapest, Johannesburg, London
or New York. This may account for their popularity for, after all,
as the slogan goes, 'You know where you are with a McDonald's'.

The world young people grow up in is not only changing
more, but also changing faster, than ever before. This makes it
hard for them to value 'old' ideas, puts them under pressure to
accept and adapt to the new, and leaves them feeling destabilised
and threatened.

Globalisation and fragmentation

The term 'Global Village' was first coined by Marshall McCluhan
in the 1960s and there is overwhelming evidence that the world is,
through mass communications, 'coming together'. But it is also
fragmenting, as people desperate for a sure identity revive age-old
tribal conflicts, as seen tragically in former Yugoslavia and in
Rwanda.

Some of us have the feeling that the greater our awareness of
the global village, the louder the clamour for our differences to be
acknowledged. Those forces of mutual need and scientific discov-
ery which tend to pull us together as human beings are balanced
by those of class, race, religion and nation which work to separate
us from each other.

Our research has shown that young people are sometimes living in a virtual reality world in which they can be anyone they
please but feel so small and insignificant in the real world that
they feel there is nothing they can do to affect their community,
nation or world for good or bad. Nothing matters, nothing is
important and no one cares.

Preparing for the peak generation

Someone has estimated that by the year 2000, 50 per cent of the
world's population will be under fifteen years old. However, this

percentage is in fact declining in the West. The year 2010 will see the peaking of the global teenage generation at an all-time high – not only the largest group of teenagers the world has seen, but the highest proportion of teenagers within society. The momentum for this great demographic wave is already building, and the commercial organisations of the world are preparing. Young people are increasingly the focus of media and marketing campaigns.

The impact of these three trends is shown in a number of different ways. For more and more young people, the Christian church is seen as belonging to the past: irrelevant to the fast-paced, morally uncertain modern world. Those from Christian families struggle to see what place the legacy of faith can play in the emerging global culture.

Call it relativism, post-modernism, pluralism or multiculturalism; whatever label you use, young people are being led increasingly to believe that everything can be true for those that want it to be, but that nothing can be objectively true enough to provide a basis for living. For the young person this results in uncertainty and a loss of truth.

Another impact of these trends is a sense of rootlessness and a loss of community. The twin forces of globalism and tribalism are bringing the world together, but at the same time tearing it apart. Young people are left, for the most part, unsure where they belong, and struggling to establish reliable, consistent relationships.

They are increasingly unsure about their purpose in life. Unemployment is a reality for many. The Careers and Education Business Partnership in Birmingham publish an annual 'Destinations' survey of school leavers in the City. In the summer of 1997, 6.9 per cent of Year 11 school leavers were unemployed (Year 11 students are aged 16). The good news is that this figure is 1 per cent down on the previous year, but the truth is, you as a parent may find your 16-year-old without work and determined to leave school. I can recall from my own experience the drive to leave school behind at the age of 16. In spite of pressure to take A levels, I left and joined the bank. The person who said that schooldays were the best of your life, was not seeing things from my angle. What do you do as a parent when your son or daughter announces they've had enough of school? How do you cope with the adolescent who never seems to get up in the morning and mopes around the house all day, watching television and drinking coke?

As part of its New Deal policy, the Government is wanting to find training for 18- to 24-year-olds who have been unemployed for more than six months. However, for teenagers leaving school at 16 or 17, there is no such scheme and parents will be expected to support their unemployed young person. Of those leaving school in Birmingham in 1997, 7.8 per cent found training places, including modern apprenticeships, whilst 9.6 per cent found employment. I understand the young person who wants to leave school and there are jobs available for 16-year-olds, many with long-term prospects. So I would urge you not to despair, or feel a failure because your child decides on this course of action. They may, after all, be following the steps you took at their age.

As part of the preparation for these years, I suggest you consider what to do if your teenager ends up without work. When times are already hard for the family, to continue to support them financially will be very difficult and the temptation will be to apply pressure to get your adolescent to get a job, any job. If they failed at school, their self-esteem and self-confidence will be low, and your pressure, however justified, could have devastating effects. In researching for this book, I spoke to the local Careers Office and found their advice and information very useful. Not only do they know the local employment situation, but they will offer advice on allowances and training opportunities. Do some research of your own so that you get an idea of what jobs are available in your area and then find an appropriate occasion to discuss this with your son or daughter. In the end you want them to go down to the Careers Office to get the information for themselves.

In spite of the temptations to the contrary, this is the time to give unconditional love, to affirm them in who they are and to build their self-confidence. It is definitely not the time to threaten them, or, worse, throw them out the home. By the way, in Birmingham, 68.7 per cent of 16-year-olds stayed on for further education of some sort (in case you're adding up my statistics, 7 per cent did not respond to the survey!).

The traditional values of job, family, home and community no longer hold true, but no workable, reliable alternatives are offered. Many young people see no 'point of entry' for their participation in adult society and feel alienated and disenfranchised.

We are in the midst of a technological revolution as pervasive as the industrial revolution, and this is shaping the way young people think and behave. Millions of young people are now post-literate, in that they relate better to images than to words and struggle to relate this to the 'book culture' of their parents.

The philosophy of materialism, expressed through consumerism, is fast becoming the defining religion of the human race, with young people being told that with the right products they can have the perfect body, the perfect relationship, the perfect family, the perfect home and the perfect life. The problem is that, unlike their parents' generation, they know that this is not true – but go along with it for want of any viable alternative. The resulting 'ache inside' is creating a worldwide spiritual crisis.

Market forces and the mass media are combining to create a global youth culture, putting young people under unprecedented pressure to conform. This is serving, in part, to deepen the generation gap, creating cultures which are 'continuous in space but discontinuous in time', meaning that young people have more in common with their peers than with their parents.

Worldwide, more and more people are turning to violence to solve insurmountable problems. This is expressed in urban violent crime, in road rage and in a proliferation of local conflicts on every continent, and is reflected, often indulgently, in films and the media. Young people are increasingly presented with the implicit suggestion that violence works as the universal problem-solver. It has been estimated that by the time children reach fourteen years of age, they will have witnessed 18,000 murders on television and countless hours of related violence, nonsense and unadulterated drivel! Psychologists are now recognising that children are affected by what they see on TV. We will remember the tragic circumstances surrounding the death of the toddler

Jamie Bulger and the real belief that those who committed the murder were adversely affected by violent video games.

One frightening statistic is that there has been a 50 per cent increase in violent crime among 11–14-year-olds in the last seven years. Parents need to be sensitive to the belief among young people that problems with relationships can be resolved through violence.

The city, for generations the great dream of mankind, in which protection and prosperity could be extended to a concentrated population, is turning, for many, into a nightmare of poverty, violence and social decay. Young people increasingly find themselves lost and alienated in an urban environment that, in many cases, doesn't even pretend any more to have anything to offer.

Local issues such as racial tensions, rising crime and social breakdown combine with global crises, such as war, AIDS, famine and environmental decay to present young people with a poisoned legacy of problems seemingly too big to solve. It is increasingly a struggle, in such circumstances, to have hope. It is small wonder that the suicide rate among teenagers has increased by over 75 per cent in the last decade. Kurt Cobain, the rock star, lead singer of Nirvana, committed suicide in 1995 and summed up his life in the lyrics of his songs: lyrics about his search for a meaning to life which he found to be an impossible exploration and his despair that in the end the quest itself was futile. His suicide note read, 'I had it all, it wasn't enough.'

In YFC, we believe that young people can make a difference and as parents you can support them to live the deliberately different lifestyle by modelling it yourselves.

These are some of the huge social changes which increasingly shape the lives of young people. They will not all be directly affected by all these changes, but many are subconsciously and indirectly shaped even by factors which do not directly touch them. Those who have no direct contact, for instance, with the victims of famine or HIV/AIDS, are confronted week by week with TV images which bring home to them the reality of these problems. Those who have neither cable nor satellite TV, and know nothing of the non-stop stream of media images flooding many homes, are nonetheless shaped by the fashions and images that spin off from the flood – children who know nothing about athletics insist on wearing 'the *right* trainers'.

Chapter 7

Sexuality

The pressures and tensions of sexual change are an inevitable feature of adolescence, and are right at the heart of the emerging adult identity. Parents need to be open and honest in this area. Talking of 'that' subject with your children can be embarrassing, but it is helpful if you do not turn a brighter shade of crimson and cough and splutter when sharing intimate details with your adolescent.

In my experience in talking about this issue with teenagers, they rarely want or welcome their parents taking the initiative. Whilst this may come as a relief to you, it is also true to say that I believe parents should be prepared to help their children especially in the area of making love as opposed to having sex. It may come as a shock to your children to learn that you still 'do it' and that you still enjoy the physical side of your relationship.

In my own family, my elder son reminded me of the mistakes I had made in this business of sex education. He took great delight in telling me how he had seen through my ruse of leaving a strategically placed book, *Just Good Friends* on the coffee table. He and his brother decided to remove said book to their rooms, in turn, on the pretence of reading it. Neither did, apparently and neither seemed to welcome my efforts at raising 'that' subject.

In addition, the problem is, very often, that sexuality is confused with sex. As children grow up they look to their role models, their parents, to affirm them in their sexuality. There are too many people who have suffered from throwaway comments about how their parents really wanted a child of the opposite sex. This has led to the child feeling they got it wrong and have been a disappointment from the day they were born. As parents of adolescents you should look to affirm (that word again) their sexuality and gender which will promote self-worth and help establish their sexual identity. All this is an essential part of growing up.

The problem is your child may well be confronted time after time by exaggerated rumours and fears, by old wives' tales and young people's gossip. What is most needed is an even and stable view, and reassurance that all is well. What you as parents want to see is your teenager making wise choices in the area of sexuality and, as Steve Chalke, the well-known writer and broadcaster, puts it:

> Even the most freewheeling parents tend to become relatively traditional when it comes to their kids and sex. It's natural for us to want to protect our children in every area of their lives, and this is doubly true in the arena of sex. Sexual decisions are the most intimate we can make. And sexual mistakes are often the most painful. In fact, it's no exaggeration to say that they can even be lethal.[13]

He then goes on to give some basic principles for guidance through this minefield. You as parents should not try and avoid the reality that many 15-year-old young women are sexually active and many 15-year-old boys would like to be. Here the general rule that girls mature faster than boys is of little comfort to their parents. But how do you provide the 'internal chastity belt'? There are three fundamental mistakes to avoid:

Avoid telling your children nothing. This leaves the door open to the innuendo, the myth and the half-truth. Remember they will be taught the mechanics but not the morals.

Avoid telling your children old wives' tales. Stories about storks, gooseberry bushes, or birds and bees may save your embarrassment but in the long run will only breed confusion.

Avoid telling your children all the graphic details. Too much information, too early in life, can be overwhelming and lead to misunderstanding. Rather try to give as much detail as you feel is appropriate at the time.

Steve Chalke then goes on to tell an amusing story:

When 6-year-old John asked his mum, 'Where did I come from?', she knew the time had come, and gave him a full biological explanation of egg, ovary, orgasm and intercourse. When she'd finished, half an hour later, John's only comment was, 'That's funny. Peter says he comes from Brighton.'[14]

Tell them bit by bit, giving as much information as seems to you appropriate at the time. Our experience as youth workers in YFC, has shown us that telling young people about sex does not push them into sexual relationships earlier than would otherwise be the case. But we do believe passionately that sex is not dirty, it is certainly not cheap and should not be given away to the first bidder but kept safe until marriage and a lifelong commitment to one person.

Statistics indicate that only 1 per cent of women getting married today are virgins and it is clear your children will be under pressure to conform. They need all your support in this area. The best and safest from of contraception is still the word, 'No'.

Some other essential strategies in this area are:

- Be aware of the struggles. Both socially and physically, young people are maturing earlier than in previous generations but are generally marrying later. This lengthens the time during which they are sexually mature but, according to a Christian morality, inactive. Ian Gregory, a BBC news producer, writes, ' "No sex before marriage" may be a novel concept, but "No sex before death" is no laughing matter.'[15] Society's answer to this dilemma has been to abandon a Christian morality, and your child will be confronted daily, in the media, with the articulation of this answer. The struggles are real and the pressures enormous – think seriously about preparing yourself now to be an effective help and support through this time.
- Keep affection flowing. The relationship between sexual promiscuity and tactile need is clinically proven: young people who feel the need for love to be expressed to them in touch are driven

to seek sexual encounters. Adolescence is not the time for parents to withhold tactile contact. Hugging may be out of order in certain public places, or in front of peers, but is very much required at home. A hug a day for maintenance is not a bad rule; though you must be sensitive to times when hugging is not wanted!

- Be ready to talk when they want to. Unfortunately this may be after midnight, sitting on the kitchen floor. Teenagers will often shrug off your attempts to discuss sexuality, saying, 'There's nothing I need to know', or, 'Don't worry, I'll tell you when I have some questions'. But at an unexpected, and probably inconvenient, moment they will want to start a conversation – at the heart of which will be a question that really matters to them. These moments are very important, and are golden relationship building times.

- Do some reading of your own. You may well know all there is to know about sex, but you probably won't know it in the adolescent context. Invest in a book or two to refresh your mind on how to explain it all, and changes to look out for.

- Remind yourself regularly of the pressure your child is under, the moodswings, the peer influence, the media hype, the fears and phobias. Remember from time to time the things you have read (or refer to this book) on developmental issues, so as to be clear in your own thinking on the stage your child has reached.

- Take a positive view of sexuality. As we have said, sex is not dirty, is not unmentionable, is not cheap, is not associated primarily with sin.

- Encourage positive peer relationships. The single greatest asset your child can have in developing a healthy understanding of their sexuality is to belong to a supportive, honest peer group. This alone is reason enough to find a strong, well-run Christian youth group for your child, even if that means allowing them to move away from the family church.

- Don't pry, interfere or be overbearing. Be close but not too close, available but not pushy, present but invisible.

- Be prepared, when the time is right, to be honest about your own sexual history; you may have come into sexual activity early or late, you may have been promiscuous or self-controlled, you may have been through an adolescent phase of homosexual attraction. Not everything will be appropriate to tell, particularly in early adolescence; but there will be times when your honesty is needed, and your vulnerability before your own child will help them enormously.

- Above all, surround this entire area of your child's life with affirmation. Their developing sexuality awakens in its turn the need to be loved, the desire to be desired. Your love and affirmation will go a long way to meeting this need. A secure relationship with you is the greatest single asset they can have in developing a healthy sexuality.

- Also, as a Christian, I believe in the power of prayer and feel that to bring this subject regularly before God is good for your security as a parent and good for the protection of your adolescents.

The following are five things that a teenager will need to know in this area:

1) They need to know that you welcome their sexual maturity and want them to feel good about their physical appearance and their developing sexuality.
2) They need to know that you want them to develop positive relationships with the opposite sex.
3) They need to give themselves permission to feel good about their sexuality.
4) They need to know that God designed the human personality so that the full expression of sexual intimacy should be reserved for marriage.
5) They need to know that they will have to draw some lines and make some clear decisions about expressing their affection and their sexuality before marriage.

One last area in which parents and supportive adults can help their children to develop a healthy attitude to their sexuality is to model wise decision making in other areas of life. Making wise choices, for example, about the use of time, money and property, teaching restraint and giving: all contribute to modelling 'deferred gratification'. It was Freud who said that the sign of maturity was to accept delayed gratification but our culture, as well as that of the adolescent, shows its immaturity by modelling instant gratification. A healthy approach to sexuality says that the best choices are based on wisdom and love, rather than on opportunity. The self-discipline which you demonstrate in your everyday life can help to prove or disprove this.

Before we move on, perhaps something needs to be said about sexual orientation. The homosexual lobby records that 10 per cent of the population are 'gay' and you may have to face this issue with your offspring. Claire Short writes this on the subject:

> In puberty and early adolescence, an attraction to another person of the same sex is, like masturbation, quite natural. After all, you know how this person acts, feels and thinks – it is easy to identify with him or with her.[16]

It is a great pity that our society no longer allows people of the same sex to share a love which is deep and profound but not romantic. One of the great friendships in history was seen between David and Jonathon and the Bible says of their relationship, 'And Jonathon had David reaffirm his oath out of love for him, because he loved him as he loved himself.' and later, 'I grieve for you Jonathon . . . Your love for me was wonderful, more wonderful than that of a woman.' There was no hint of homosexuality about their friendship. Short goes on to write:

> If your child has had the courage to share with you, 'Mum (or Dad), I think I'm gay!' try not to dismiss their concern with comments like, 'Of course you're not!' or 'How could you do this to us?!' Instead, endeavour to listen with understanding, and explore with your child the reasons why he or she has come to that conclusion. I have known several situations where parents take on misplaced guilt, blaming themselves for 'getting it wrong'. These parents often need more help coming to terms with the situation than their adolescent.[17]

As a parent the first thing you will have to deal with is any feeling of guilt. Almost inevitably you will ask yourselves if you are in any way responsible for your child turning out 'differently'. Blaming yourself is not very helpful and the reality is no one really knows what leads people to become homosexual. There is little known about teenage male homosexuality in general and even less about adolescent lesbians. What is true, however, is that the 'gay' lobby has been so successful that, in spite of this lack of knowledge, The House of Commons voted by an over-whelming majority to reduce the age of consent from 18 to 16 years of age. However, at the time of writing, the House of Lords have voted against this reduction in the age of consent and it will not, as a result, become law as part of the Criminal Justice Act. The Government did not wish to delay the rest of the Bill to include this measure. However, in the Queen's Speech in November 1998, they stated their intention to introduce a Bill to lower the age of homosexual consent to 16.

It is helpful to understand that most young people go through an anxious period in their lives when they wonder, 'Am I gay?' This often happens around the age of 13 or 14 when young people will admit that they find a friend of the same sex attractive, or they develop a crush on a teacher of the same gender, or they engage in some homosexual activity. What is in fact happening is that adolescents are establishing their own sexual identity. As we have pointed out: the adolescent years are the years in which the whole identity of the person is evolving and this is part of that evolutionary process. It is not one of which many of us are proud when we look back to our own teenage years but, if we are honest, we remember the struggles. By doing this memory exercise, we can help our own young people cope with this period in their lives.

None of this suggests that the person is homosexual or will become homosexual as an adult. It is therefore important not to attach labels to our own children as they form their own sexual identity. But what do you do if, by late teens your boy or girl defines him or herself as a homosexual?

Firstly they are not mentally ill. Whilst many religious groups consider the homosexual lifestyle to be immoral and contrary to nature, it is the church which should be in a position to love and accept all people. Sadly this is not usually the case. Tony Campolo berated the Lambeth Conference in 1998:

> You amaze me, you Anglicans. You have bishops who deny the deity of Jesus Christ but you don't split. You have bishops who deny the resurrection but you don't split. You have bishops who deny the inspiration and authority of scripture but you don't split. But you're ready to split over this [homosexuality]? No wonder the world calls you homophobic.

Secondly, then, you must accept them, not reject them. Your youngsters will be wrestling with this issue and will be afraid to 'come out' due to the social stigma attached to homosexuality, the fear of bullying and 'gay bashing', and the concern they have as to how you, their parents, will react. They still need you.

This will not come easily to you. The lost dreams of your child marrying and having a traditional family, coupled with your own negative stereotypes of homosexuality, may take some working through. She or he is still your daughter or your son and you should channel your energy into providing love and support. Most researchers agree that your child did not choose homosexuality but, as has already been stated, there is too little knowledge on the subject to be categorical. However, what is certain is that they will undoubtedly experience rejection. Your acceptance of them and your willingness to talk things through will enable you to discuss frankly the risks of such a lifestyle and even suggest some counselling.

Thirdly, do not blame yourself. You cannot take the blame for the choice your son or daughter has made. It is all too easy to feel that you as a parent have made some dreadful and long-lasting mistake in the way you have brought up your child which has resulted in him or her becoming homosexual. There is no one factor identified as the root cause of homosexuality.

Finally, on this subject of risks, the same applies to homosexual practices as to heterosexual ones. There is no such thing as safe sex. Young gay men are one of the fastest growing groups for new HIV infections. Since 1982 there have been 3,878 cases of HIV infection among young gay and bisexual men aged between 15 and 24 in this country. This represents 12 per cent of all HIV infection. There is only safety in abstinence.

As parents you must give unconditional love and realise that orientation is not the same as practice and it is the latter which the Bible condemns. By supporting our children and responding with loving concern, they will have every chance of emerging with wholesome and confident sexual identities.

Culture, Change and Sexuality are three of the landmarks that are inevitable on your journey. If you face no other issues in your preparation, face these three.

There are other important landmarks you need to take into account as you plan the route through these years, and it is to these I now turn.

Chapter 8

Conflict

Rob Parsons of 'Care for the Family' was speaking at Spring Harvest in 1998 and mentioned something which we feel is very important as we look at this question of conflict. 'Adam and Eve had the most perfect parent and yet they still messed things up!' You as parents will sometimes fail. Conflict may end in tears and your adolescent may kick over the traces but you must not carry guilt, it is not your fault or failing: it is the choice of the emerging adult.

During adolescence an adult personality is emerging, being born. It is inevitable that this personality will test itself against those closest to it, assessing its own strength, finding out where the limits are. Parent/child conflict is inevitable and unavoidable but it is not something new. I was fascinated to read in a book published in 1802, consisting of extracts and articles from the Methodist Magazine for that year, a letter from a mother to her daughter:

My truly dear Nancy,
The more I reflect on your unexpected requeſt to let you go to the concert, the more I am averſe to a compliance. You ſay, – 'It is only muſic.' I grant it. But can you or I conſcientiouſly agree to this thing, when we reflect on the certainty of its being unprofitable to the ſoul? Can you expect to meet God there? Is there any promiſe in Scripture that gives you ſuch a hope? But ſay, my dear child, Do you go with that intent? Is it your motive for going? Whether we eat or drink, or whatever we do, we ſhould do all to the glory of God.[18]

The language is a little quaint, but the truth is that conflict between the generations has always been with us. However, the truth remains that if handled well it will promote health for all concerned. Some helpful things to remember are:

- Know that you're being tested: this is not a real war (yet!). Choose the right battles to fight. Jim Graham, Pastor with Ministerial Responsibilities at Gold Hill Baptist Church told us that he and his wife tried to major on the majors, rather than major on minors. He said that they did not consider clothes or hairstyles major issues and whilst this meant that their sons sometimes looked, to all intents and purposes, like young thugs this was OK because they knew their hearts. We shall look at some of the issues we consider worth fighting later on.
- Check your own reactions. Are you dealing with an issue of parental discipline, or is it hurt pride, ego or self-defence?
- Set out some guidelines, if necessary, through a 'family council' meeting. These can be adjusted as your teenagers get older and prove they can be trusted.
- As soon as possible take the initiative to defuse the situation. Leave them to cool off. Avoid being the one to escalate conflict.
- Practise forgiveness, both in your own heart and with your mouth.
- Be willing to apologise in any area, even the smallest, in which you are in the wrong; your apology sends a signal of honesty and the willingness to lay down arms. Try to be the first to apologise, even if you do not feel you have done or said anything wrong. Just by saying something like, 'Sorry I reacted in that way but what you did (or said) really hurt me', can be a signal that hostilities are at an end.

Someone once said that you can always tell a Christian home: they close the windows before shouting at the children!

But what are the areas where a strong stance is required and the battle lines need to be drawn? Whilst these will, to a certain extent, differ with every family, we believe the following need to have your close attention:

House rules
Under this heading there are probably four areas which seem to cause the most problems, both to parents and to teenagers. These are: coming home late, fashion, chores, untidy bedrooms and parties. Let's look at them in turn.

Coming home late

Coming in late after a night out is probably the most common subject for disagreement between parents and their adolescent children. It sums up all the things they dislike about teenagers. Parents think that if young people come home late they are selfish and unthinking, only interested in having a good time and careless about their own safety.

Of course, from the young people's point of view things look a bit different. They may feel their parents have been unreasonable and have given them no room for negotiation about deadlines. They may even have tried to get home on time but were held up by things beyond their control. Some young people may feel that staying out late is the only way they can force their parents to recognise that they need to be given more independence. And sometimes they're just plain thoughtless – we all are at times.

The problems are often exacerbated by the fact that when they do come home late they are tired and you are tired, fed up and feeling angry. Hard as it may seem, banning certain friends and activities, or grounding your teenager, rarely changes the behaviour patterns and you may be sentencing yourself to long evenings with a stroppy young person stomping around the house. Our research has shown that stopping pocket money is both painful and effective, but a solution which both parents and young people find works best is to stay calm and listen to the young person's point of view, while still showing how upset you are. We believe that negotiation is the best way forward to find a compromise which is acceptable to both parties!

One further point before I give some practical suggestions. In *The Sunday Times* of 30 August 1998, it was reported that David Blunkett, the Education Secretary, was going to instruct schools to make agreements with parents setting basic rules for behaviour, time-keeping and homework. Bedtime rules, for example, would be introduced based on research which indicates that children aged between 8 and 11 need eight to ten hours sleep each night, while with puberty, the amount of sleep needed can go up to eleven hours. However, surveys show that about half of 11- and 12-year-olds stay up to at least 10 p.m. Mr Blunkett said:

> We recognise that we can't enforce bedtimes. But it does matter and it is an example of where schools can provide encouragement and guidance, because there are parents who are not sure what is expected.

So, here are some guidelines for this vexed issue of coming home late:

- Let them suggest a time to come home – they often stick to their own deadlines.
- If you have your own transport, offer to pick them up at an agreed time (maybe round the corner from the party or cinema, so that you won't embarrass them in front of their friends).
- Invest in a phonecard to make calling home easier.
- Suggest inviting friends home sometimes instead of always going out.

Don't be afraid to adapt rules, it doesn't mean you're caving in. It shows you're trying to trust them more and respecting their point of view. In return they will respect you more.

Fashion

As Jim Graham said during an interview for the parenting seminars which form the basis of this book, 'We did not consider clothes a major issue. They are not a matter of life and death!' But fashion can cause problems for parents, especially when it comes to clothes being too revealing and jewellery being attached to unusual parts of the body. You must be aware that sometimes your daughter or son may simply be wanting to shock you, or perhaps wanting to make a statement that says, 'I'm different from you lot and I'm trying to find my own identity.'

Of course, they may also be wanting to look like their friends. As has already been said, peer pressure is very strong in the teenage years. Fashions change, fortunately, and sometimes it's good to get out some old photographs of when you were a teenager, to remind you of flares, miniskirts and kipper ties! You still need to give advice about the clothes suitable for certain occasions, particularly for such things as job interviews. And remember, many adults go to great lengths to continue looking like teenagers!

Chores

I think it is perfectly reasonable to expect some help with the domestic chores but it is best to come to some agreement in advance as to what is fair. This is especially true when it comes to sibling rivalry, where the cry is often heard, 'You don't make him do it. It's not fair!' What does not work is for a tired and irritable parent to suddenly announce that it is time the young person did something to help. To hope that the teenager will obediently jump up and start the washing-up, or do the ironing under such circumstances is unrealistic.

- It may be a bind but sitting down with the family and together drawing up a rota of tasks for *all* the members of the household, will go a long way to resolve this accusation of unfairness.

- You could also suggest that pocket money is earned by certain chores being completed around the house. If you hate ironing, an agreed figure for your son to do his own will benefit him in the long run and ease your own burden.

Untidy bedrooms

If you feel you need a tetanus injection to enter your child's bedroom, do not despair, you are one in a long line of parents who have found this a flashpoint in their relationship with their teenager. Private space means a lot to adolescents and there may be more worthwhile things to insist on than whether your daughter or son keeps a tidy room. Studying for exams, keeping healthy, or safe from harm is probably more important than tidiness and, after all, they have to live in it, not you, and if you really can't bear it, ask them to shut the door! But you can insist that trashing the communal living space is unacceptable behaviour.

I suggest:

- You agree not to invade their bedroom, so long as they don't mess up the rest of the house.
- You agree you will knock on their door before entering the bedroom, as long as they respect the same privacy with your bedroom.
- You insist that anything they take up into their bedroom (mugs, plates, etc.) must be brought out again, preferably before it has grown its own culture!
- You seriously consider their request for a lock on the bedroom door and certainly on the bathroom door.

Parties

I was blessed with two sons who were not party animals. This meant that the vexed question of parties and all the possible grounds for disagreement was not one which Val and I had to face. Even when Andy was eighteen he did not want a party, but he and some school friends who had formed a band, put on a 'gig' for their mates in the church hall. Big brother was invited, together with some older twenty-somethings, to act as 'bouncers', just in case. However, I know from talking with many parents that they did not escape so lightly.

Our next-door neighbour confided in us that her daughter wanted a party to celebrate the end of GCSEs but that she and her husband were really concerned and wondered what they should do. The problem, it seemed, stemmed from the fact that, whilst they felt they could trust their daughter, it was the possible gate-crashers which caused the party to be put on hold. Obviously she did not want her parents to be around and cramping everyone's style, but they did not feel able to allow that much freedom. An outing to McDonald's was no longer an option!

The situation was complicated by the fact that one of their daughter's school friends had held such a party, only for it to end in disaster, when a group of 'lads' not invited to the party started throwing stones, one of which smashed a window and someone was badly cut from the broken glass.

Now, I know many parties are held with no such unpleasant results and I certainly do not wish to be alarmist. The story simply serves to illustrate the thinking of parents and just one or two of the various factors you will have to consider when faced with this question. I have not even begun to talk about alcohol, cigarettes, invitations, number of guests, noise, neighbours and what to do if things get out of hand. One of the most discussed topics always seems to be whether parents should go out for the night or stay in to ensure everything is orderly.

If you have a good relationship with your teenager most of these things can be resolved to everyone's satisfaction and it is a further sign that you are giving your daughter or son more trust and responsibility. I really cannot give you a hard and fast set of rules and regulations to follow but I do recommend that you try not to allow the discussions to degenerate into a stalemate. Keep the options open for as long as possible. But in the end, it is your house and your child and if you do not feel comfortable with the party arrangements, you must say 'No'.

Sexual relationships

I would love to be able to say this will not be a problem for children from a Christian home, or for children whose parents have strong moral standards. However, in *Quadrant*, published by the Christian Research Association (CRA) in Autumn 1997, it was reported that a Harris survey for the Oasis Trust in 1997 showed that 1 in 2 of all teenagers claimed to have had sexual intercourse before the age of sixteen. CRA's own findings among young people who go to church show that a Christian upbringing does have a positive influence on sexual behaviour, with just 12 per cent of those questioned claiming to have had sexual intercourse. This compares with 18 per cent of those questioned in 1991 – an improvement which may have something to do with AIDS, but equally may be to do with a greater willingness on the part of Christian young people to take a stand against declining moral standards.

As youth workers, we in YFC believe in taking a biblical approach to sexual relations which, it must be said, contrasts with the general view taken by such organisations as the Trust for the Study of Adolescents. The view that you, as a parent, must not try to impose your values and must allow them to learn from sexual mistakes, is not very helpful.

We believe that sexual activity should be kept for marriage and that God intended for two people to become one for a life-long union. We feel that God's command to flee sexual immorality just shows his understanding of our human frailty. This does not mean we will judge or condemn anyone who does not fit neatly into this package. We are all human and none of us is immune to the power of sexual attraction.

So what should you do as a parent to help your adolescent? I suggest the following:

- That just as you taught your children to say, 'No!' to strangers, they should use the same technique with a person who wants them to have sex.
- That to abstain from sex means they will be protected from guilt.
- That to abstain from sex means no unwanted pregnancies.
- That to abstain from sex means no sexually transmitted diseases.
- That to abstain from sex means protection from emotional distress and provision for true and lasting intimacy.

In all this your teenagers will have to find their own levels. Discussion of 'How far can we go?' is common among youth groups. Steve Chalke puts it simply like this, 'Don't touch what you haven't got!' But this is a time for sexual experimentation amongst adolescents and auto-eroticism starts with masturbation. The old adage is probably true, 'Nine out of ten lads do, the tenth is a liar.' We in YFC do not advocate it but neither do we condemn it. What we do say to you as parents is, be prepared to talk to your teenagers in an adult, unembarrassed way, and guide them through these years when their sex drive is reaching its peak.

One mother came to me and asked, 'What should I do? I found *Playboy* magazine under the mattress of my 14-year-old son. Should I be angry at the exploitation of women or simply pleased he's not gay?'

I'm sure many mothers have similar stories to tell about their sons. All our research leads us to believe it is mainly boys rather than girls who are aroused by looking at the naked forms of the opposite sex. This interest in experimentation is a natural part of the young man's growing into sexual maturity. In today's culture, many young people cannot wait to grow up and try out their 'new' bodies and what the young man is doing is testing out the bits he can, to see if they are functioning yet. It is the image of the woman that excites him rather than the fact it is a woman. He is also wanting to see what a woman looks like, in the flesh. Mothers will often react in different ways from fathers and this reflects the different ways women and men view sex.

Women are aroused by feelings, by touch, by sensitivity, by tenderness, and by talk of love and commitment. Men are aroused by looking, by thinking and by doing. This generalisation helps you as a parent talk to your son. Bring out the fact that feelings and emotions are important in the sexual relationship. It's not just sex. Women are not objects like something you buy in a supermarket but they have feelings and needs which, in good relationships, are just as important to the man as the woman he loves.

One 18-year-old told us:

> I didn't see that sleeping with him was wrong at the time. I was sixteen when I first met him and was really happy. He was nineteen and pushy. For the first few months we had a very physical relationship. I wasn't that bothered as my friends were sleeping together and I wasn't that committed as a Christian. I first slept with him when I was seventeen. It did feel wrong the first time but he told me it was OK and I thought he knew what he was talking about. My friend at school told me not to worry. I was just scared he wouldn't go out with me if I didn't sleep with him.

Your teenage daughter may never tell you she is sleeping with her boyfriend; it takes a great deal of courage to own up to something of which she knows you will disapprove. If you have always had a good relationship which has stood the test of time and she knows you will be upset but not angry with her, then she may share her secret. To break up from such a deep involvement with a young man will need your support. She will be lonely, especially if it has been an exclusive relationship and she has lost other friends. She will almost certainly feel guilty about a number of things and your understanding will be a comfort to her. Please try to avoid the temptation to patronise by saying something like, 'There are plenty more fish in the sea'!

We understand there is an experiment in Tyneside to reduce teenage pregnancies which involves handing out contraceptives to girls of 13 and 14. Whilst we agree it is better to do something rather than nothing at all, this is a matter of morality and demonstrates the acceptance that our society has no absolutes – all is relative. As I have said, we in YFC believe that young people need to be given absolute values which include moral ones and we certainly teach this when we are in schools. Furthermore, in spite of the millions of pounds spent on health education, contraceptive services and counsellors, teenage conceptions, which fell considerably in 1975 when contraception became freely available on the NHS, have risen for 11 of the last 15 years.

It is refreshing to hear Health Minister Tessa Jowell saying, 'Having sex at 12 or 13 robs you of your childhood and it is the job of parents and teachers to safeguard childhood.' In other words, you as parents can help by not trying to get your children to grow up too soon.

Drugs

As a youth leader I was surprised to be told by the group at the church that they considered it easier to get hold of drugs than it was to get alcohol. They knew who to go to. Most young people will have been offered drugs and some will have used them. About one third of young people in this country will have used cannabis by the age of 16 but less than 5 per cent will be experimenting with substances such as crack or heroin. Some 9 per cent of 15-year-olds admitted to using solvents (sniffing glue, lighter fuel, tippex, etc.) or having used them in the past. Most young people who take drugs do so out of curiosity, boredom, or peer pressure and continue misusing drugs through a combination of factors ranging from enjoyment to physical and psychological dependence.

The CRA survey mentioned earlier, showed that 13 per cent of young people going to church and aged 16 to 17 had taken an illegal drug and, overall, 7 per cent of those aged 11 to 19 had used drugs. As with sexual activity, these are encouraging statistics as they show the influence you have as parents. However, I do not believe you should be simply relying on the fact that your children have been brought up in a good home, as sufficient to ensure they do not experiment with drugs. My prayer is that you will not need any of the following advice and information but I consider it is part of my brief to you as parents to give you some guidance in this area. Colin Piper talked to young people on this issue. He was told:

> I thought it was rubbish after the first time but didn't feel guilty. I guess I felt it was all right because I was drinking at the time and felt it was the same really. The second time I did it because it was there and I couldn't see what was wrong with it. I didn't reason it through. Dad found us and walked off. Later he told me, 'If I find them with drugs again, I'll throw them off the premises'.

Another young person said,

> At a party the house can be full of drugs. Schools and colleges are full of them too. They're all around you. They're at the clubs you go to, everywhere. Lots of my friends are tripping. People say it doesn't do any harm.

A Government White Paper, published in April 1998, *Tackling Drugs to Build a Better Britain* includes a personal statement from the Prime Minister, Tony Blair:

> The fight against drugs should be part of a wider range of policies to renew our communities and ensure decent opportunities are available to all. We are tackling inequalities through the largest ever programme to get people off benefit and into work and a series of reforms in the welfare state, education, health, criminal justice and the economy.
>
> But that is not enough. I am determined to tackle the drugs problem. That is why I appointed Keith Hellawell as the first ever UK Anti-Drugs Co-ordinator to put together a comprehensive strategy, coming at the problem afresh.
>
> The strategy is an important step. But the fight is not just for Government. It is for teachers, parents, community groups, those working in the field and everyone who cares about the future of our society. We owe it to our children to come up with a truly imaginative solution to create the better Britain they deserve.

The Government's strategy has four elements:

YOUNG PEOPLE – to help young people resist drug misuse in order to achieve their full potential in society.

COMMUNITIES – to protect our communities from drug-related anti-social and criminal behaviour.

TREATMENT – to enable people with drug problems to overcome them and live healthy and crime-free lives.

AVAILABILITY – to stifle the availability of illegal drugs on our streets.

In reading the White Paper it became clear that parents are expected to play their part in becoming better informed about drugs generally. I consider it not just a matter of being informed but taking a more positive approach to drug education. Josh McDowell, the well-known speaker and representative for Campus Crusade for Christ, in his book, *Right from Wrong*[19] takes parents to task for abdicating their responsibilities. He writes that we have delegated to the Sunday School teacher the task of teaching our children about Jesus, we have delegated to the youth worker the task of teaching our children about sexuality and we have delegated to the dayschool teacher the task of teaching our teenagers right from wrong.

He believes that parents have the responsibility to know and teach their children about drugs. How can you do this? I would recommend a publication called *Action* produced by Hope UK (the address is in the Appendix) and the publications from the Department of Health called *Drugs – a Parent's guide* and *Solvents – a Parent's guide*. These can be obtained through Hope UK or Her Majesty's Stationery Office. YFC has produced a video and workbook called *More than a Feeling* which can be obtained from our Head Office. All of these publications will help you to understand the role you can play in fighting the illegal use of drugs.

But what else can you do to educate yourself and your children about drugs? The truth is probably that your son or daughter will know more about the subject than you do having been given some drug education at school. However, you can help your child most of all by setting a good example in the use of drugs at home. The Department of Health give two examples and you may wish to think of additional ones which are appropriate to your own situation.

> Mum might explain why she takes painkillers when she has a period. Dad might explain that he likes a drink with his friends, but never drives afterwards. Therefore, it is important to explain *why* we are taking the drugs we do and what we feel is appropriate or inappropriate drug use. This process can start when children are quite young and it needs to continue throughout childhood and adolescence.[20]

Your part then is to be better informed and to be good role models for your children, but you also need to know when your teenager is experimenting with drugs, to recognise the signs and to know what action to take. There are a number of signs that teenagers may be regularly using drugs:

- sudden and irregular mood swings
- lack of interest in their friends
- gradual loss of interest in school, hobbies and sport
- difficulty concentrating
- unusual tiredness or drowsiness
- increased evidence of secretive behaviour
- loss of appetite
- money or other objects missing from home
- unusual aggression
- unusual stains, marks or smells on the body or clothes or around the house.

But tread carefully, there could be another explanation altogether innocent.

Remember

- Never ignore a drugs problem – all illegal drugs, including cannabis, can be hazardous. Act immediately.

- Do find out what your teenager is taking and how often.
- Do your homework – know what you're talking about. Get professional advice if necessary (see Appendix for helpful agencies).
- Don't panic or threaten to throw them out.
- Do point out the dangers calmly – even so-called soft drugs may result in a criminal record.
- Do make sure your teenager knows they have your support.

Chapter 9

Handling Conflict

Are there rules for dealing with conflict? Isn't it better to back off and do nothing in the belief in 'anything for a quiet life'? Let's take a look at a senario which is very familiar in today's Christian family.

When they no longer want to come to church

In April 1991 the evening celebration at Spring Harvest was interrupted by hundreds of teenagers coming into the Big Top from every entrance, chanting and dancing. Scores of them got onto the stage: it was all rather disturbing; I could not work out what was going on. They certainly made their presence felt. Suddenly, at a given signal all the teenagers fell silent, turned and filed out.

A representative of Youth for Christ addressed the Spring Harvest guests, 'There were three hundred teenagers in that group, we really notice their absence, don't we? That's the number leaving the church every week. Yes, every week.' There was hardly a dry eye in the place. It certainly had a profound effect upon me and led me to a deeper involvement with YFC.

Such statistics, produced by Dr Peter Brierley of The Christian Research Association, really hit home when it is one of your teenagers who has decided to leave the church. As part of the preparation for parenting adolescents, it is helpful to consider what to do when your child states they are no longer coming to church. I am afraid it's happening all too frequently, and whilst I would like to spend some time in examining the reasons why, others have written in a very helpful way on this subject, notably Andy Hickford in *Essential Youth*[21] and David Cohen and Stephen Gaukroger in *How to Close Your Church in a Decade*.[22]

What I want to do is give some practical advice at this point, having drawn on some research among other Christian parents who have been through it, and got the tee shirt and the video! One mother in our church in Bromsgrove told me how she longed for all her children to become Christians and had never stopped praying to that end. One was in his forties before he came to give his life to Jesus, and she had prayed every day for him. Such dedication pays off, so don't despair, nor feel you are a failure; after all, the bottom line is: it's their decision.

There are those who take a very high view of church theologically and would want to put it ahead of the family in order of priority. The family, they point out, is not the primary means of God's grace, it is the church that holds this place of honour. However, in a culture where the family is under such pressure that even the Government is looking to find ways to support the family, it is good to remind ourselves that the family remains God's model for building a community in which everyone is included. As the psalmist says, God is the father of the fatherless, defender of widows and the one who places the lonely in families. Gary Collins' book *I believe in the Family*[23] is a useful resource if you want to look into these issues more.

My task, as I've said, is to be as practical as possible. When I talked to young people about the benefits and problems of being brought up in a Christian home, most said the good things outweighed the not so good. Interestingly though they often put it in terms like, 'There were not so many rows as some of my friends have to put up with.' Another regular response was that the Christian home was more secure. There was another side to their comments which is worth reflecting upon. 'I don't find it easy to talk about my faith at home though. My parents never talk about their faith with each other. They'll talk about lots of other stuff, like school, boyfriends, even TV, but never about their personal faith.'

I have quoted Jim Graham as saying that he tried to discern the major issues from the minor ones, and did not consider certain things like hairstyles to be life-threatening. There is no doubt that as Christians we would consider rejection of the faith as life-threatening, and as such, you as concerned parents can start now to address the issues. Someone has said that there is no such concept as grandchildren in the Kingdom of God, all are children, which means all of us must have a first-hand experience of Jesus, not one passed on to us by our parents.

So begin now to talk about your faith in front of the children. As I have said, teenagers are looking for a faith that works, and if they see and experience that in their home, it is more likely to be caught. Openly demonstrate your love for Jesus by putting your faith into action. I remember having a conversation with my sons about the fact that they reckoned I only did what they termed 'good deeds' to make me feel better. We were able to share together what really was my motivation.

This leads me to my second point. At a time when young people will be questioning many things as their mental capacity develops, it is important that they feel they can raise questions of faith at home. The problem is we tend to think of questions as challenging our stated point of view, but this is not necessarily the case. Questions can be seen as the desire for clarification. When I worked at the bank I taught marketing skills, and as part of the course we looked at the area of objections raised by the customer. Often these could be viewed as positive, and never to be taken personally.

Your adolescent will be taught things at school which may be diametrically opposed to your Christian views and standards, and which he may have accepted without question until challenged in this way. By encouraging questions, you will help him firm up his own faith.

A third point to make at this stage is that you have to allow your daughter or son the freedom to find their own faith. By removing some of the pressure to follow in your ways, and by not assuming she or he is a Christian can, in the opinions of the young people themselves, allow them the space to establish a real personal faith.

It can still come as quite a blow when your child declares they are not coming to church with you. What do you do then? I do not believe you can force them to attend church, indeed, I am sure this is counter-productive in the long run. If anything is going to drive you to prayer this is it!

First of all I think there needs to be dialogue. Do not be surprised if the announcement, 'I'm not coming' is made just as you are about to leave for church. Now is not the time to enter into an argument: you will end up at worship in completely the wrong frame of mind. It's best to indicate that you agree for the moment but that you would like a discussion later. It is important that you try to establish the reason for the refusal, endeavouring not to treat it like a rebellion and the start of civil war.

In the present-day society it is definitely not cool to go to church, and rather than risk the taunts of school friends, it's easier not to go to church at all. In this case, the young person does not feel they have to live a lie. I am sure you would rather they were honest and acted with integrity, than continue to go along with your wishes whilst feeling hypocritical. Some good friends of mine told me of the occasion their daughter said she was not getting up to come to church. 'I'm not interested in what you're interested in', she declared. After the initial shock (their two older children were strong in the faith) they decided to back off and not make a fuss.

'However, we kept asking her to various things we thought she would be happy with, and she surprised us on several occasions by agreeing to come. We never put her under pressure,' they told me, 'and she will come on Christmas day with the family.'

I wondered if they had thought of going to a different church with more lively worship, or with lots of young people. 'No,' they replied, 'With the other two older children being so settled in the church, it makes that quite difficult. Unless the whole family decided, we feel we have to dismiss that idea.'

For some of you reading this, you may want to consider trying other churches for the sake of the children, but I would make sure that it is your church that is the problem, not simply that your child is no longer interested. If your teenager wants to explore the faith and your church is boring and irrelevant, in their eyes, then it may be time to look for a credible alternative.

My friends were also willing to stay away from church on occasions to be with their daughter at home, to demonstrate their love and affirmation of her. It has also been exciting to witness the continued friendship of young people from the church for this teenager, whose other friends have come and gone.

I certainly agree with my friends' approach. I feel that to enter into an argument every Sunday as you try and persuade a recalcitrant adolescent to join you in church, can result in total impasse, where they harden their attitude more and more, in direct proportion to your attempts to break their resistance. One 14-year-old asked me, 'Why does there have to be conflict about going to church? There's only conflict if the parents insist on their teenagers going to church. If they allow them to make up their own minds and encourage them to go, it's much better in my view. At my church I'm made to feel involved by being given jobs to do, so I'm happy to go along.'

Equally, in these days of reductions in extra-curricular activities at school, it could simply be that your child wants to play sport on a Sunday morning, as this is the only time available for 'Little-Leagues', or swimming, gymnastics or ballet. By entering into a calm discussion, these things can be established and they open the door for negotiation. If, for example, you allow them to carry out the activity of their choice, then you would expect them to come with you to church one or two times each month in the evening. You know the situation in your church and the negotiation will need to be tailored accordingly.

This may be the first time your adolescent has had the opportunity to negotiate with you so be careful not to patronise them.

I sincerely wish that church were the most exciting place for young people, but the reality is that many find it really difficult. It's not surprising when I hear so many criticisms of church from adults. We in Youth for Christ recognise the need for experiments in youth congregations and for credible youth events. Unfortunately our resources do not allow us to have a centre in every town and city in Britain. There are many other good organisations putting on youth events. If you can find committed young people who will invite your daughter or son to go along, then this could become church until your prayers are answered and your children find their own faith.

Having looked at a specific situation and how to deal with its potential conflict, let us look at the wide issue in a more general way.

The following are six principles for dealing with conflict:

- Avoid personal insults. Your children can cope with you saying they can do better, can turn that C into a B, that B into an A, but they can't handle you saying that they're no good, they're stupid and they're a failure. Your children will begin to believe it for themselves and fall into the classic self-fulfilling prophecies.
- Stick to the matter in hand. Don't drag into the argument all the other times when you have felt let down.
- Remember the power of the tongue. The Bible likens it to the power of a rudder to steer a ship.
- Remember the power of 'sorry'. The silliest statement to come out of Hollywood was, 'Love means never having to say you're sorry'. On the contrary, love means always having to say you're sorry.
- Recognise that conscience is on your side. If you have set down family principles before the teenage years, these will be working for you during adolescence.
- Remember the power of forgiveness. We have all been forgiven at one time or other and know how good it feels to be restored.

Unfortunately it is not good for you or your teenager to avoid conflict at all costs. You may want the quiet life but you could end up doing more harm than good.

- It may stop the relationship from deepening and developing.
- It may stop the child from facing problems and dealing with them in an effective way.

- It may allow the child to manipulate you through your giving in.
- It may damage your self-esteem as parents.

Dr Ross Campbell has some helpful advice on how to deal with anger. He writes:

> Many parents assume that anger in a teenager is bad or abnormal, and that expression of it should be suppressed or not allowed. This is a dangerous error. One of the most important areas in which a teenager needs training is in how to handle anger. The feeling of anger is not bad or good in itself. Anger is normal and occurs in every human being. The problem is not the anger itself but in managing it. This is where most people have problems. I believe it is *imperative* to understand the different ways to handle anger and know which ways are best.[24]

There is insufficient space to go into the full detail of Campbell's argument but he believes that it is possible to train a teenager in handling anger. The major problem parents have with anger is that they do not differentiate between anger that is appropriate and that which is inappropriate. This leads to the feeling that the young person is being disrespectful. You need to know that most teenagers have a respectful attitude to their parents. Equally you need to know that the more they put their anger into words the better it is. Anger in any human interaction is bound to occur and if not dealt with will tend to build up to an explosion. Here as the adult parent you can do so much to nip the anger in the bud by getting the young person to talk about their feelings and deal with them in an appropriate way.

Campbell sets out what he calls the Anger Ladder where only the top two rungs are totally positive. Describing the different levels of maturity in expressing anger is very complex. Campbell shows fifteen ways of behaving while angry and you will notice that most expressions of anger are primarily negative.

1. Pleasant behaviour
2. Seeking resolution

 3. Focusing anger on source only
 4. Holding to the primary complaint
 5. Thinking logically and constructively
 6. Unpleasant and loud behaviour
 7. Cursing
 8. Displacing anger to sources other than the original
 9. Expressing unrelated complaints
10. Throwing objects
11. Destroying property
12. Verbal abuse
13. Emotionally destructive behaviour
14. Physical abuse
15. Passive-aggressive behaviour[25]

It is important that you affirm your daughter or son in expressing their anger verbally. After all, you want to know when they are happy and the times when they are sad. It is right that they let you know when they're angry. You can then tell them you're proud of the way they handled their anger: they didn't kick the cat, they didn't thump their little sister, they didn't throw anything or even slam the door. Next time, you'd really be pleased if they didn't drag up that old chestnut about not being allowed to have a party when you're away.

Please remember this is a long-term project and in the process, you as a parent will learn as well. As I have indicated already, adolescence is an extended period and throughout it teenagers need to learn those social and relational skills which will stand them in good stead in adulthood.

And finally, remember, never invite trouble, it will accept the invitation every time!

Chapter 10

Crisis in the Family – Divorce

'Why did my dad divorce me after he divorced my mother?' This question, or ones similar to it are often heard by YFC workers when talking with young people about their experiences of divorce. All too often young people are kept in the dark by parents who are experiencing problems in their marriage and when the news is broken, this is the type of comment we hear, 'It was obvious something serious was happening. Things had begun to go rapidly downhill between my parents. However nobody told us. We felt like we didn't exist.'

One young person asked, 'Why did God think up families?' Now as a Christian I firmly believe, as I've already said, that as Psalm 68 puts it, God is the father to the fatherless and that his ideal is for the lonely to be set in families. But I also realise that living together in today's 'pressure-cooker' culture can prove too much for some married couples, who decide, for the greater good of all concerned, that it would be better to live apart.

Of course parents try to protect their children from the difficulties they are going through. The young people who spoke to us felt a mixture of shock, hurt, anger, pain and rejection coupled with a dash of relief, once the announcement had been made that their parents were to divorce. Many felt that things should have been explained to them but they understood that their parents were hoping, against hope, that the situation would improve. It was good to hear from many that once the initial emotions were released and the situation began to take on a sense of normality, it was possible to find some light.

This chapter obviously deals with a very specific subject which some of you may consider has little relevance to you. I do not apologise for including divorce in a book on preparing to parent teenagers because, whilst I feel passionately about marriage, I am realistic enough to know that none of us is immune to the possibility of marital breakdown. So, as part of your preparation and to avoid the dangers of not thinking through the implications of parenting when the going gets tough, may I suggest you do give some time to this section.

I have been concerned in researching for this book to concentrate on the effects of divorce on young people. As with other sections I have included the comments of young people to help you as a parent see things from their point of view.

In a paper published by the Family Policy Studies Centre in October 1997, for example, it simply states that Home Office research shows that the effect of parental conflict and broken families is one of the major factors in youth crime. It goes on to say that research also shows that pre-divorce factors, especially financial hardship, play an important part in explaining why, as adults, children whose parents divorce have an increased likelihood of lacking qualifications or being unemployed.

Furthermore, women whose parents have divorced are more likely to give birth as single or cohabiting mothers. Another disturbing finding is that those who experience the divorce of their parents during childhood are more likely to see their own partnership or marriage breakup than those whose parents stay together. Apparently no one is asking what makes marriage work and relationships survive!

Tony Blair said in September 1997:

We cannot say we want a strong and secure society when we ignore its very foundation: family life. This is not about preaching to individuals about their private lives. It is addressing a huge social problem. Attitudes have changed. The world has changed but I am a modern man leading a modern country and this is a modern crisis.

I give you this pledge. Every area of this Government's policy will be scrutinised to see how it affects family life. Every policy examined, every initiative tested, to see how we strengthen our families and you will have a ministerial group to drive it through. We cannot do it all on our own but I believe Government should play its part.[26]

What is the nature of the crisis? Here is a set of statistics to put the matter in perspective. These are from the Family Policy Studies Centre paper mentioned above.

- There are approximately 16 million families in Britain.
- Four out of five families are headed by a married couple.
- The vast majority of young people (85 per cent) aged 16 to 24 live in a family.
- Just under one in ten adults is in a cohabiting relationship, although this rises to one in five among younger age groups.
- Two in five marriages are predicted to end in divorce.
- Seven in ten divorcing couples have children.
- Over a third of births are now outside marriage.
- Just over 7 per cent of all families with dependent children are stepfamilies.

What is clear is that family life as we knew it is no longer the way it will look in the next century. People have asked what are the reasons for the increased rate of divorce in Britain and the Western world generally. Many point to the Divorce Reform Act of 1969, which came into force in 1971, and the 1994 Matrimonial and Family Proceedings Act which have led to couples being able to file for divorce after their first wedding anniversary, if there has been an 'irretrievable breakdown of marriage'. New legislation allows for the 'no fault' divorce to be available.

I was encouraged to learn that the divorce rate was beginning to slow down until I read the statistic that the number of marriages in the United Kingdom has fallen by 25 per cent in the twenty years between 1975 and 1995.

However, I believe there is a more subtle reason behind the divorce rate and here I move onto more controversial ground. Whilst I am pleased to read the speech of Tony Blair quoted above, I recognise this as an attempt to counterbalance the forces which have been undermining family life.

In 1978, P. Abrams wrote, '. . . one of the plainest and firmest findings of sociological research is that the family remains the strongest and most highly valued basis of social attachment UK society possesses'.[27]

By 1982, the feminist movement saw the family as 'the pivot of oppressive socialisation' and saw the cultural norms which structured the relationships between men and women with respect to marriage, childcare, care of elderly relatives and domestic labour within the family as gender stereotyping, creating subordination for women and girls and freedom for men and boys. The family, according to the feminist movement, is the most significant transmitter of gender stereotypes and is the main enemy. This oppressive socialisation of women within the family is mirrored and reinforced by other institutions in society, particularly the school, the job market and the church.

Now please understand I am not blaming women for the demise of family values in the United Kingdom but I am saying that the things undermining the family are more subtle. Nor am I advocating a return to the 'kitchen sink' for women with children. What I do believe is that the clamour for freedom from the family structures that feminists have articulated so strongly in the past, needs to be examined in the light of research into the outcomes of divorce on children and young people. The assumption that it is really all right whether the parents are together or not, that no particular form of family structure is better than another, has now proved false and, indeed, deeply destructive.

I believe the church needs to put out different signals. It needs to affirm women as individuals and their place in leadership, whilst at the same time, modelling strong family structures. It is in the church where those who are hurting, those who have been divorced, those who are single parents, should find the greatest understanding, love and support. My fear is that this is not the case. Too often the church excludes women and alienates single parents. However, one of the things I think the church is good at is the marriage preparation undertaken by many clergy. Research shows that this reduces divorce.

Feminism has, quite rightly, made us review our thinking and I have been made to relearn my vocabulary. Not to say I am politically correct all the time but I have learned that when talking of a managerial vacancy in YFC, I must not talk about 'he' who will fill the post, or 'she' who will be the new secretary. I am pleased to say that YFC is working towards being an equal opportunities employer and has a policy on the egalitarian acceptance of women in leadership (our Position Paper on Women in Leadership is available from our Head Office).

The Joseph Rowntree Foundation published a report called *Divorce and separation: the outcomes for children* in June 1998 which came to four major conclusions:

- Parental separation is most usefully viewed as part of a process beginning before divorce itself and continuing long after. Support may be needed and intervention required at any stage to reduce possible detrimental effects on children.
- Although short-term distress at the time of separation is common, this usually fades with time and long-term adverse outcomes typically apply only to a minority of children experiencing the separation of their parents.
- However, these children have roughly twice the probability of experiencing specific poor outcomes in the long term compared with those in intact families.
- Some widely held views about separation are not supported by the evidence:

  - the absence of a parent figure is not the most influential feature of separation for children's development;
  - the age at which children experience separation is not in itself important;
  - boys are not more adversely affected than girls.[28]

What can we learn from the young people who travel down the road of divorce with their parents? Christine, an 18-year-old, told us:

My work suffered and my grades dropped. I couldn't be bothered and became very apathetic to work. I didn't talk to my friends. They just knew we had problems. I worked on a need to know basis. I didn't talk to anyone which was one of my biggest mistakes. I have very mixed emotions like a shaken champagne bottle. The cork will give at some point. It's made me cynical, sarcastic, harder and tougher. I have a brick wall around me which mustn't come down. I'm quite comfortable as I am. I feel safe. I can't see myself married. What if I picked the wrong person or the wrong person picked me? I don't let people close enough.

From this one conversation alone a number of problems can be identified which most young people face in the time when their parents are also going through really hard times. What seems to happen is that, quite understandably, parents get caught up in their own spiral of difficulties and, to survive, become inwardly focused. Communication with their partner has sunk to the level of shouting, or slanging matches, or sulking and it seems all reasonable discussion is impossible. This leads to so much stress that such parents simply cannot focus on anyone else but themselves. I know it must be hard but teenage children do want to know what is going on. As I have said, the vast majority of those we have spoken with felt they should have been taken into the confidence of their parents.

'At first I blamed myself because I thought they'd argued and split up over something I'd said.' This is fairly typical of the comments we heard.

First of all then, I would urge you to take your adolescent children into your confidence. Because you are finding it almost impossible to talk to your partner it does not follow that you have to withdraw from your children. They take this to mean they have done something wrong, that it is they who are causing you, the parents, the very problem which you are always arguing about and many carry this guilt into adulthood. You may want to reply to this by pointing out that your teenager simply breezes in and out of the home, treating it like the proverbial hotel, and seems totally oblivious to what is going on. I would want to respond by saying that, in my experience, it is the very fact that the home is a secure place which enables them to treat it in this way. You will be surprised how sensitive they are to mood changes and 'atmosphere'.

Secondly I advise you to listen to their questions carefully. They will be anxious to know what caused the split, whether it is permanent or whether there is a chance of you getting it together again. The questions may all come tumbling out in one go but, depending on the characters of your children, they may want to take time to consider the things they want to ask. You can help by understanding what is going on from their point of view. They will want to know if you are going to marry someone else. They will be bewildered by the process and will suddenly become very insecure. 'Where shall I live, who will I be living with and can I still see the rest of the family (grandparents, uncles, aunts etc.)?' These will be very important points of clarification for them and the sooner it's talked about the better for them.

Try to be honest and straightforward in your responses and re-member, you may have fallen out of love with your partner but it is unlikely that your children will have. They can do without your slandering your spouse.

So it's really about communication but it is also about being sensitive to their mood swings as well. We have looked at the changes young people are facing in the teenage years and by add-ing another pretty drastic twist to their lives by your separation and divorce, will result in your children finding it hard to cope on some days. As Christine put it, 'My work suffered and my grades dropped.'

Thirdly, then, I would suggest you consider taking your child's Form Tutor or Head of Year into your confidence. Do this only with the agreement of your daughter or son but there is not the stigma attached to divorce that there once was, and by letting the school know in this way will give your child more understanding from the teaching staff. By answering your children's questions you will enable them to tell their friends what is going on at home and, hopefully, the cloak of secrecy will be lifted. The shaken-up champagne bottle with the cork about to burst is a good meta-phor for how many feel. Allowing the subject to be discussed freely and openly should result in the bottle being replaced in the wine rack for some celebration at a later date.

'I wondered what I had done to make my dad stop loving me and my mum and my sister.' This simple statement leads me on to my fourth point. Your adolescents need to know that you still love them. You may be receiving signals that they no longer need your love or, even worse, reject it but, as Sophie told Colin Piper, 'When we say we don't want a hug we really do.' At this time there is an increased need for your love. Young people's vulnerability can be seen from the questions they ask. Now, as never before, show them unconditional love.

This is not a book about marriage and I will not presume to try and moralise in any way. I do want you to know that if you are experiencing marriage difficulties, guilt will not be far away and that is the enemy of making a fresh start. The failed ideal does not mean you are a failure. Alys Swan-Jackson, a freelance journalist, quotes Louise, a 16-year-old, and I'll let her have the final comment:

> Even though things have been bad, I don't think I've ever regretted my parents getting divorced. They never could get along. The rows were awful. It's better without all that. Sure, I wish they could have been more friendly, but things turned out different. The best thing to come out of it is that Mum and I are much closer than we used to be. We get on really well. Getting divorced is not the end of the world, it hasn't put me off marriage, but I hope I never have to go through it myself.[29]

Chapter 11

Bullying

There can also be times of crisis for your children of which you should be aware and I want to look particularly at bullying. I was surprised to read from a survey carried out by Peter Smith and Irene Whitney, published in 1993, that bullying in primary schools is worse than in secondary schools. Some 27 per cent of pupils reported bullying more than twice a term compared with 10 per cent respectively.[30] Now this may be the result of a certain amount of bravado on the part of older students who do not like to admit to being bullied but the truth is all schools have some bullying. Whilst most schools now are making every effort to deal with bullying, you must play your part in helping your children handle it. One girl from Battersea, quoted in *Youth a Part* said,

> At my school, being an all-girls school, there were loads of bullies, and if you weren't with the bullies you were on the other side, and I didn't want to be on either side so I bunked school.[31]

What is bullying? It is a form of aggressive behaviour which is usually hurtful and deliberate; it is often persistent, sometimes continuing over a number of weeks, months or even years and it is difficult for those being bullied to defend themselves. Underlying most bullying behaviour is an abuse of power and a desire to intimidate and dominate. Whilst it can take many forms the most common are physical, verbal and indirect.

I suppose all of us will have joined in the childish chant, 'Sticks and stones may break my bones but names will never hurt me.'

This simply is not true. The bluff is as poor as the rhyme. Physical bullying is fairly obvious and involves hitting another person or damaging their property. One of the disturbing side effects of television and cinema has been the increase in kicking seen in the playgrounds of schools. YFC workers have witnessed the inexorable rise in martial arts-style kicking which forms a regular part of play and bullying behaviour.

Name-calling and general insulting and teasing of other students forms verbal but still very hurtful bullying. When this includes racist or sexist remarks the hurt can be even deeper. To be called 'Paki', 'Wog' or 'Cow' is not funny. I was interested to find in talking to the young people in my youth group that the term, 'Swot' was not one which young men ever wanted to be called. Apparently anyone who shows an aptitude for a subject, especially if he is a boy, is likely to be branded a swot. This is not good news and may account for the significant discrepancy between the examination achievements of boys and girls. Girls are beginning to outshine their male counterparts in GCSE and A level results, highlighted by the publication of school league tables by the Government.

One 17-year-old spoke to me about the treatment he received because he wanted to work hard and was bullied as a result. He told me:

> It's hard to describe as it is how you feel, it [bullying] takes many forms really. It goes from like name-calling to physical violence to exclusion. There is a lot more than you think. People think if they talk about it, it will probably get worse. It happens that if people start saying things about having friends that it will happen to them as well. Then those bullying get their friends to back each other up.
>
> I was quite fortunate in the fact that I actually lived a fair bit away from the school in the opposite direction so it was kind of hard for them to follow. In my case it was 90 per cent of my year and it seemed like everybody was against me. In fact most people. It made me feel very lonely and like you get depressed.
>
> The school tried to get a bullying policy but it was not really successful for reasons that basically, a lot of the time, it is one voice

against ten or twenty. Bullies rely on people not speaking out don't they?

I told tutors but had a feeling of being left on my own.

Indirect bullying can be more subtle but still very damaging. This takes the form of spreading nasty rumours and excluding someone from social groups. Girls are more likely to be involved in this form of bullying where 'to send someone to Coventry' can have a lasting effect upon another's self-esteem, especially where the exclusion appears irrational and unwarranted.

The effects of bullying can make a young person's life really miserable. If your adolescent child is injured and the cause seems suspicious, or begins to be unhappy about going to school, you may need to try to ascertain if bullying is the reason. Without action being taken, young people will lose self-confidence and self-esteem and blame themselves for inviting bullying behaviour. Concentration will suffer and so will the ability to learn. Physical symptoms may result from bullying, such as stomach-aches, headaches, nightmares or anxiety attacks. In the long term, persistently bullied children are more likely to become depressed as adults.

As I have already said, the good news is that almost every school in the country is taking bullying seriously and those which are most effective are often the ones to which parents choose to send their children. However, young people are often reluctant to tell anyone they are being bullied. When you discover that your child is being bullied they may try to persuade you not to approach the school, but a barrier of silence will only perpetuate the problem. Most young people we spoke to do not like bullying but are reluctant to talk about it in any detail.

It may be difficult for your youngster but I want to encourage you to talk to the school if you consider your child is the subject of bullying. As I say, schools are wanting to deal with this anti-social behaviour and many have well-defined strategies for dealing with the problem. I am sure you, as a parent, will be shown a copy of the school's bullying policy which will include how and to whom to report such allegations.

You as parents can help to reduce the possibility that your own son or daughter may bully others by ensuring that you do not use position or power to achieve your own ends. Children who regularly hear how their parents manipulate other people into doing something to further their own aims, may be encouraged to try similar tactics in school.

You can also help your adolescent by teaching some assertiveness techniques. I believe that the best place for dealing with bullying is the school but you, as a parent, can help by advising your teenager to have a strategy, not to be afraid to ask for help and support and to be ready to walk away from difficult situations as quickly as possible.

In the book *Tackling Bullying in Your School*[32] edited by Sonia Sharp and Peter K. Smith, the writers give some helpful advice on how to be assertive. The following points summarise their ideas:

1. The non-verbal messages

Assertiveness techniques are a mixture of messages, some of which are picked up by the potential bully without your child even opening her mouth. When acting assertively she should not slouch but try to look the other person in the eye. Now is not the time to smile or laugh or cry, but the facial expression should convey confidence. Avoid body language which can be seen as aggressive such as crossed arms, or hands on hips. Hands can be put in pockets as a sign of a relaxed attitude and this will prevent any signals such as pointing.

2. Verbal messages

Assertive messages should be delivered without raising the voice but simply and honestly stating how you feel about the circumstances. For instance, it is often difficult for conscientious students to work while a lot of noise is going on The right verbal message would be something like, 'I would like you to be quiet', rather than, 'Belt up or I'll slap you!' To do nothing is to suffer, in silence. The right verbal message can work in cases of mild physical aggression.

3. The cracked-record technique

It is not always easy for young people to simply say 'No', especially if they have been brought up in a Christian home where they are taught to be 'nice' which can lead them into doing things they really don't want to. It can be hard to stand up to a barrage of threats such as 'I'll split on you', 'I won't be your best friend any more', 'Chicken! What a wimp!', or 'Go on, this'll be the only time' and resist. One way of resisting is to use a technique known as the cracked-record. Here is an imaginary dialogue:

Becky	Lend us a quid, Fiona.
Fiona	I don't lend money.
Becky	Oh go on, I'll pay you back.
Fiona	I don't lend money.
Becky	But I lent you some the other week.
Fiona	I don't lend money.
Becky	I won't let you borrow any of my CDs ever again!
Fiona	That's a real shame, Becky, I like your *Oasis* single but I don't lend money.
Becky	I give up!

Research shows that the person usually gives up after three attempts but the technique is also effective when the one being bullied walks away at the appropriate time.

4. Sticks and stones will break my bones but names . . .

We all know that name-calling hurts, as I've already said. One of the ways to help stop this is called 'fogging'. When fogging, the person being bullied replies in a way that is aimed to defuse the situation. 'You might think so', 'Possibly', 'It might look that way to you' and 'So' are fogging-type statements. The name-caller will hopefully become tired if the taunts are seen to be having little effect.

It is important to understand that this technique is not effective where there is more than one person doing the name-calling. Here it is best not to respond verbally but to internalise positive statements such as 'I am going to be cool' or 'I am proud to be me'. Parents can be of enormous help to their children by not calling them names at any time. To say to your son that he is stupid or your daughter that she is fat is in itself a form of bullying.

5. Get help

Emphasise that if your adolescent is being bullied they do not have to sort it all out by themselves. At the very time when you as a parent may be trying to empower your teenager to stand on their own two feet and make grown-up decisions, it may be necessary to teach them that, on occasions, calling for help may be the appropriate action. All of us rely upon others to a smaller or greater extent all the time, and this does not devalue us in any way. Learning our place in the whole scheme of things is an important part of growing into adulthood.

6. Get out of there!

It must be said that, especially for boys, the whole male/macho thing may prevent them from seeking help and support, or from walking away from the bully. Nevertheless, it remains the strong thing to do and you as a parent can instil this into your children. It is the strong thing to do because, taking a stand and not retaliating will, in the long run, be of benefit to others if the bully can be stopped. It also teaches a valuable lesson that taking matters into your own hands where bullying behaviour is concerned is not the best solution in adulthood either. If your children have learned the techniques in adolescence they will be in a good position to know how to handle the aggressive behaviour of work colleagues and bosses.

7. Build their confidence

These techniques have their place but the most effective deterrent to bullying remains the building up of your child's self-esteem. If your child is on the receiving end of statements from his parents that he is not good enough, or is failing to live up to the standards set, then the classic self-fulfilling prophecy can so easily set in and he may well fail. If, on the other hand, he is happy with who he is and is regularly affirmed by you and valued simply for who he is, his self-confidence will remain, even in the face of close encounters of the bullying kind: name-calling, nasty looks and attempts to exclude him from the group.

Chapter 12

Values You Will Need

Before looking in detail at the values you will need as a parent of adolescents, I believe it would be helpful to provide a simple framework within which to operate by using the mnemonic *TALK*:

Take an interest. It is imperative during adolescence that your children are aware that you are interested in them. It will not be easy but by keeping the channels of communication open and showing you care about what they're doing will help you to know when crises are developing in their life and in your relationship. Don't be put off by the grunt in reply. For a teenage boy whose voice is wavering between soprano and baritone, it can be embarrassing to hold a lengthy conversation!

Without interfering or being overbearing, begin to take an interest in the music, films, sports, fashions and celebrities your children are keen on. Borrow the Walkman and listen to a tape or two, in their presence if possible! Let them know, as a basic rule, that what interests them interests you – not as a member of the secret police but as a fellow human being. Make plans to do things together. Jim Graham tells of the time he took one of his sons to the speedway and skipped an elders' meeting to do so! There are activities which your whole family may enjoy together, like going to the cinema or out for a meal to celebrate an anniversary, or simply sitting down to play a 'silly game' together, which does not cost anything. Let your children see your enthusiasm for pleasure and entertainment.

Affirm the Good. Too often the only time a father is heard to say, 'Well done' is when ordering a steak. Children love attention, but they learn very early on that if they're good they're ignored, so guess what? They are naughty to gain the attention of their parents. This trait can continue well into adolescence if, when they are good, parents do not affirm them and simply ignore their best efforts. We consider that children in their teens need to have the good affirmed in them just as regularly as the toddler who takes its first steps, or says its first words.

You should be looking to congratulate them on good time-keeping, good control of money, good choice of friends and just general all-round goodness. There is nothing that will take the steam out of potential conflict more effectively than pre-emptive positive action! Also find good in your teenagers' tastes and interests, and encourage them even if they are outside your personal taste. It will be far less painful, when the time comes, to make a stand against things which really are unacceptable, if you have been positive about things which are acceptable and it will give you the capacity to suggest alternatives Make a personal choice not to get caught up in the hype that labels all youth culture as sinful and dangerous.

Look before you leap. One of the traps that is all too easy to fall into is painting oneself into a corner by coming out with a statement such as, 'If you don't stop using all the hot water every morning with your wretched baths, you'll not stay under this roof.' Such a trivial matter may get blown up out of all proportion and neither you nor your adolescent may be willing to back down with the result they actually do leave home. The relationship might never recover. Look before you leap. The same is true about culture. Discerning good and bad in culture requires more than a superficial analysis – it requires time and consideration. If you are concerned about a given cultural form or activity, take the time to look more closely. Talk to other parents, to youth specialists, to teachers and church leaders. Read reviews and other literature. By examining an issue more closely, you will learn more; you will be more likely to make a wise choice, and you will be modelling, all the time, the type of critical choice which you are asking your child to make.

Know why the bad is bad. When you find areas of danger in youth culture (and there are many!), be prepared to say why you feel as you do without sounding off too much. What are the specific dangers? Why is this an influence you would rather your child avoided? Be honest about your fears and positive about your love for your child. By doing this you are helping your child to understand and you are making it clear that you are not criticising or attacking them. Sometimes they will be glad of the opportunity, and ammunition, to resist peer pressure. Campbell in *How to Really Love Your Teenager*, gives some good advice on the subject of peer pressure.

As a parent he was often faced with difficult questions especially when it came to going out to parties. He tried to get as much information as possible to make a decision but if he felt there was something of a hidden agenda he would play for time. He would offer the answer every salesman hates, 'Let me think it over!' He recounts the time his daughter was happy to use his refusal which enabled her to withdraw from a situation she felt uncomfortable about. Somehow it is possible for young people to resist peer pressure and to maintain their credibility with their friends by saying, 'My dad won't let me.' At other times, they will fight you anyway, but at least you will know that you stand on solid ground!

If you have a faith of your own, then it will concern you to know if your child will follow suit. Faith is one of the basic values you as a Christian will need. Be ready to explain what you believe and why, but also prepared to be challenged. You are not God, and your teenage child may well be perversely driven to proving it! There is no doubt that however much we want to pass on our faith by teaching or preaching at our young people, they will in fact learn more from the culture in which they live. If you have cultivated a working faith in your family then this is the sort of faith which will be caught rather than taught.

Some while ago I was given a plaque which still sits in my study even though my sons have left home. It reads:

A child often criticised
may learn to condemn.
If exposed to hostility
may learn to fight.
If exposed to ridicule
may grow in shyness.
If exposed to shame
may grow in guilt.
Let us through tolerance
teach him patience.
Through encouragement
teach him confidence.
Through fairness
teach him justice.
To give a child security
is to give him faith.
And to give him love
is to give him God.

You are watching them, but they are watching you. Your example will have more effect and be longer lasting than all your talking, and in later life they will remember only that which they saw worked out in your daily life. As Eugene Peterson puts it in *The Message*, 'Don't become so well-adjusted to your culture that you fit into it without even thinking. Instead, fix your attention on God' (Rom. 12:2).[33] Where your words are matched by life and action, they will sink in. Where they are not, they will be summarily rejected. Your teenagers will be looking for a faith which works and will quickly let you know where they feel you are being hypocritical.

Young people need to be part of a living community if they are to see faith for what it is. This is one of the most challenging areas for Christian parents. Too often churches fail to include young people in their thinking and planning.

When I first became involved in the youth work at our church in Bromsgrove, the young people met on a Sunday morning in the kitchen. It was November, there was no heating and we sat in our overcoats trying to hold a serious discussion against the noise of the Sunday School J-Team, practising Christmas Carols. Only a matter of seven years earlier, the church had been rebuilt, without any provision for youth work. I am pleased to say that the leadership of the church allowed us to convert another part of the premises for exclusive use by the youth, but it highlights a common problem.

Most young people seek a group to belong to whose values they can accept and keep. If you are encouraging them to build faith, help them find a faith-building group. This may even mean you have to allow them to go to another church. It is important for young people struggling with belonging and with how to be part of a larger group, to attend events such as Spring Harvest or Soul Survivor. Here they will find themselves in the majority and with others who are really going on with God.

Tough questions will always do more for faith than easy answers; young people who never express their doubts end up ruled by them. Give them room to ask. Many young people struggle with the hard questions we all face but in the atmosphere of the modern education system they will be taught secular views about creation, philosophy, science and religion. If they go to tertiary education, there will be a whole new set of questions they will face and a whole new culture to deal with. If your son or daughter is already an integrated part of a positive peer group they will cope with the pressures far better.

The only true, reliable means of creating, developing or sustaining faith is by experience. One of the best gifts you can give to your children is the opportunity, on terms which they understand, to put their growing faith to work. In YFC, we believe passionately in providing young people with opportunities to put their faith into action. Through our 'Operation Gideon' programme we have trained hundreds of young people in youth work and discipleship in the last ten years. We now have young people giving a year to creative arts teams: using music, theatre and dance to communicate their faith. Their stories tell us how effective these programmes are both in developing the young people themselves and reaching others with the Good News in a relevant way.

Part of your plan for effectiveness in preparing to parent teenagers is about deciding what values you will carry through the process as a concerned adult, and as a family group. Getting these values right, strengthening the areas in which you are weak, and letting the family know what the core values are, will all contribute to the stability of your boat as it hits the rapids ahead. Your values make up your profile as a leader and leadership is exactly what you are exercising as you guide your family through these times. What you are doing is launching your teenager into the world with the right equipment for the journey and we will be looking at this in greater depth in Stage 3.

'I won't go into the water until I can swim!' someone said and this totally illogical statement is the opposite of what you want to do for your children but no matter how ill-equipped you feel they are, they will need to establish their own place in the world if they are to be truly adult. As Thomas Babington, a nineteenth-century politician said, 'If men are to wait for liberty till they become wise, they may indeed wait for ever.' By having a clear set of values, however, you will be providing a good foundation on which your young adults can build. We consider the following six core values will form a sound basis:

Order

We live in a diverse, varied, complex, noisy, over-stimulating, information-soaked world. Your children are presented with a plethora of opportunities, challenges and choices. What will help them to face these choices is the order your family brings into their lives. This includes the boundaries you set and the patterns and traditions you establish together. It includes the freedoms you allow, the risks you are prepared to take and the responsibilities you allocate. The theologian Francis Schaeffer described God's pattern for humanity as 'freedom within form'. And order within a family establishes this same pattern. Tony Campolo, in the interview he did for the parenting seminars, explained:

A study was carried out in the USA at Columbia University asking students graduating from high school (that is aged 18), 'What do you wish your parents had done for you that they did not do?' The overwhelming answer was, 'We wish our parents had established more rules for us.' They always felt, interestingly enough, that the parents who did not establish rules, didn't really love them very much. The responses were incredible like, 'I wondered whether my parents really loved me. I mean they didn't really care what I said, they didn't care what I did, they didn't care where I went, they didn't care about anything. They didn't care about me at all.' You see, instead of seeing lack of rules as an expression of love and trust, they saw it as an absence of love. You show you love your child by establishing parameters for behaviour.

Mission

Many young people grow up completely lacking any sense of mission and purpose, and ache with the question 'Why am I alive?' Family life can instil in them a sense of purpose, a thirst for adventure, a desire to make a difference to the world. The question 'What do you want to be when you grow up?' should not just be about economic activity but about values and personality and about the contribution your child will make to the history of the world. Young people often feel they can make no difference to the world but Tony Campolo is adamant that parents can instil a sense of mission in their children. He talks of the Jewish mother who is asked by another, 'What lovely children, how old are they?' The mother replies, 'The doctor is four, the lawyer is three!'

Campolo goes on to say:

From the time the child is an infant it is made to believe it can do incredible things. It's no wonder the Jews produce more Nobel Prize winners than any other group, their mothers believe they can do these amazing things. I taught Jewish students at the University of Pennsylvania and one of them mockingly said to me, 'No wonder Jesus thought he was the Messiah, he had a Jewish mother!'

Time

Young people understand fully that the things that matter to you are the things you put time into. If shaping your children's lives is a priority, then this must show in the way you order your life. As a guiding rule, most people in the modern world will spend less time with their adolescents than they should, unless they make a deliberate decision to the contrary and work really hard not to allow other 'more important' things to squeeze out the time allocation. You can still be an absentee parent, however, even if you are at home, if your mind is really elsewhere.

Of course many of you will spend great deal of time at work, but no one ever said on their deathbed, 'I wish I had spent more time at work'. There was a time when my sons were small when I did not see them from one weekend to the next. I was working in London, commuting an hour's journey each way, getting into the office by 8 o'clock in the morning and not leaving until 6 o'clock in the evening. One of the things Val decided to do was bring James and Andy to my place of work. This became a regular adventure. In the summer they would picnic in one of the Royal Parks and watch the Changing of the Guard. In the winter the excursion would include Christmas shopping at Hamley's and admiring the lights in Oxford Street and Regent Street.

Even now they are adults, they still wanted to see where I work with YFC and the offices in Halesowen. I recommend that you find time to take your teenagers to see where you work. Do not be afraid to let them into your world. By doing so you will be giving them time to enter into the place where you spend a great deal of your time.

Touch

Touch is a difficult subject in some circles, and practices vary from family to family, but adolescents need it more than ever. The tactile expression of affection is a deep human need, which surfaces dramatically during adolescence, when children need assurance and security. A child lacks the experience necessary to form an accurate opinion of himself, so his only guide is the reaction he provokes in others. He passively accepts the judgements which are communicated by words, gestures and deeds. As the child grows, the number of times he is affirmed by touch, by 'stroking' as some psychiatrists term it, decreases, but the need remains. The adolescent may react to a lack of touch in one of two ways: firstly by withdrawing into a make-believe world of solitude or by living out the 'bad little boy' script he feels is his identity. Both these lead to despair.

The second reaction may be to seek the approval of friends by being eager, willing and compliant. They are committed to a life of mountain climbing, constantly striving for bigger and better approbation. The problem is that there is always another mountain to climb. That is why I advise you to make hugging a habit as early as possible!

Identity

Adolescence is about the emergence of a new adult identity, which is continuous with the identity of the child but contains and opens up many new things. All people need their identity affirmed, but never more so than at this fragile stage. Affirmation is saying to a person 'You are valued for who you are: you are unique and special, and the world is a better place for your presence in it'.

One of the ways to affirm their identity is, every now and again, to spend an evening with the family photo album. This shows that you care about their development and their identity. It will also allow you to recall happy occasions and perhaps not so happy ones, whilst at the same time enjoying laughing together. When Val and I were celebrating our 25th wedding anniversary, James and Andy insisted on getting out the slides and reliving their childhood from the earliest days.

The reverse message says to your children that the planet would be better off without them. Both messages can be communicated by words and actions, and both will be picked up loud and clear by the super-sensitive emotions of teenagers. Learn to affirm, and purge your family of destructive, sniping criticism.

Unconditional love

The value which holds all these together is that of unconditional love. Your child needs to know that no matter what the future holds, no matter what moral and behavioural choices he or she makes, no matter what crises you go through as a family, you are committed in a bond of love and forgiveness. They will only know it if you both say it and, when the pressure mounts, prove it. Your calling to love your child is a high calling, and takes precedence over your role as teacher, preacher and moral guide. In other words, unconditional love makes no demands, no performance levels, no judgements – no matter what.

Margery Williams has a lovely picture of what it is to be loved in her book *The Velveteen Rabbit*, in which she writes of a conversation between the Rabbit and the Skin Horse in a child's nursery. They discuss what it is to be real and the Skin Horse explains that this has nothing to do with the way it is made but it is something which happens after some considerable time:

> 'That's why it doesn't happen to people who break easily, or have sharp edges, or have to be carefully kept. Generally, by the time you are REAL, most of your hair has been loved off, and your eyes drop off, and you get loose in the joints and very shabby. But these things don't matter at all because once you are REAL you can't be ugly, except to people who don't understand.'[34]

Conclusion to Stage 2: Planning the Route

Key Points (i)

Landmarks you will meet on this journey:

Culture   Take a balanced view, know why bad is bad and good is good.

Change   Be aware of the social revolution in which your children are growing help them to cope with life on shifting sands.

Sexuality   Don't panic! Be honest, available, affirming and affectionate! Give them 'inner permission' to feel good about themselves.

Conflict   Be ready to handle conflict. Learn to listen, defuse the situation by being the first to say, 'Sorry'.

Crises   Expect them and be prepared. Remember the TALK framework.

Faith   Live your faith to the full and lead by example. Foster positive peer relationships.

Key Points (ii)

Values you will need along the way:

Order   Set Boundaries: freedom within form.

Mission   Why am I alive?

Time   Spend it on what matters most.

Touch   Making hugging a habit.

Identity   Let me be me and you be you!

Unconditional Love   'You can always come home!'

Stage 3

Packing for the Journey

Chapter 13

Formulating Vision

In the last section, I want to get down to specific things that you can do in advance of your child's adolescence in order to be more fully prepared. These are actions that you can take immediately. You are now aware of the landscape through which you and your children will be travelling, the process of change affecting the whole family and the opportunity this gives for you as a parent to provide roots and wings. You also know that planning the route is important as you negotiate culture, conflict and crises, as well as the burgeoning sexuality of your child. There is a way through.

In this final stage, we want to show you the essentials to pack for the journey.

Many businesses today, and for that matter, charities and churches, have a mission statement, which attempts to capture in a sentence or two the vision the directors and leaders have for the organisation. Certainly most businesses will have corporate goals and objectives. But in our experience, families rarely consider and certainly very few put into writing their mission statement of vision and purpose for their children. We recommend you create two mission statements, each of between five and ten points: the first to describe what you want to be and do as a parent, the second what you want for your children.

In our interview with Tony Campolo he recommends that parents take a more positive approach to their children's future. He says:

You're letting the television say what a child should do, what to be, what to become. The school counsellor sits down with the student and charts out the future. Parents are afraid to chart out the future. Case in point: I did a study on parents in conjunction with the Fisher Associates of New York. It was done for the commercial world but the findings were incredible. We interviewed mothers from various parts of the world. When Japanese mothers were asked, 'What do you want your children to be when they grow up?', the answer was 'Successful'. No society drives its children like the Japanese but the parents know what they want their children to become – successful. If you were to ask American parents and, for that matter, parents in the United Kingdom, 'What do you want your children to be when they grow up?', you will get one standard answer, 'We want our children to be *happy*'. What a terrible mission statement, that a parent should say 'Happy'.

He goes on to say that he was brought up 'Italian' and how his parents didn't really care if he was happy. He says that if you had asked his parents the same question they would have said, 'We want our children to be *good*'. He continues:

That's an interesting word isn't it? We want him to be a good person. Is there a difference between a society that has as its mission statement for its children, 'success', a society that has a mission statement that says 'happy' is the goal, and a society that says 'good'? You see very often 'good' and 'happy' don't go together. You may be married and become sexually attracted to someone at work and you figure it would make you very *happy* to spend a night with that person. But it's not a *good* thing to do. So, I think there needs to be a mission statement.[35]

Søren Kierkegaard, the Danish philosopher, reckoned that we define ourselves in contrast and contrastedness, by which he means we all need something firm against which we define ourselves in either a positive or a negative way. Your role as a parent is to establish a firm sense of purpose for your children so they know why they were brought into this world. Now they may rebel against this definition, as we have already indicated, but that should not stop us prescribing the definition.

So much for the theory: let's now get more down to earth. In his usual practical fashion, Rob Parsons, the internationally known speaker on family issues, recommends 10 goals for busy parents:[36]

Goal 1: To Seize the Day (Every day spent with your children matters – try not to miss one of them.)

Goal 2: To Dispel the Illusions (That I can't spend time with my children, because I have no choice, because I'm too busy, because I can easily wait for a slower day.)

Goal 3: To Give Love Without Strings.

Goal 4: To Praise My Children (Catch them doing something right.)

Goal 5: To Laugh More With My Children.

Goal 6: To Set Boundaries.

Goal 7: Not to Delegate the Big Issues.

Goal 8: To Rediscover the Ordinary.

Goal 9: To Forge a Strong Relationship with my Children.

Goal 10: To be Able to Let Go.

Your mission statement as a parent may include some of these, or you might want to tackle other areas. You could, for example, start by taking this book and highlighting areas of particular relevance to you which can then be translated into personal goals. Make sure your goals are understandable, measurable and, above all, achievable.

Turning now to the second part, the mission objectives for your children's lives, these might be more far-reaching, but just as important as your personal goals. Some examples of goals in this area are:

To shape good decision makers.

To create Christian disciples.

To instil moral values.

To see my children forging, and keeping, good peer relationships.

To train good parents for the future.

To ensure that my children have a viable 'skill for life'.
To shape adults who will care for the poor and disadvantaged of
the world.

It is important that these goals, too, are achievable and measurable, and that you think through some of the practical implications. If these are effective goals, then you will find yourself,
almost before the ink is dry, thinking of ways to see them fulfilled.
You must always remember, of course, that your children will
choose whether to pursue these goals. In part this may depend on
how well you have reflected their character, rather than your
own, in the goals you have formed for them.

Chapter 14

Making Rules

I believe that the other side of the coin from formulating vision is making rules. In our research among young people we were surprised to discover, as I said earlier, that when asking students graduating from university what they would have liked their parents to do which they did not do, the answer came, 'We wish our parents had established more rules for us'. They felt, interestingly enough, that the parent who did not establish rules, did not really love them very much.

When we took our church youth group to Stoneleigh Bible Week I borrowed a minibus to transport them. It was soon evident, before we even set off, that the journey would have its trials. However, it was the wearing of seat belts that seemed to cause the most antagonism. I am convinced that none of the young people give a second thought to wearing seat belts in the family car but in front of their mates it was a different matter. It was, apparently, considered 'hard' not to wear seat belts. Now, I'm a not miserable old killjoy, at least not all the time. It would have been far easier just to say that it was fine if they didn't want to wear them and simply get on our way. But two things nagged my mind. The first was the thought of irate parents who would not appreciate my lackadaisical approach to safety and the other was the knowledge that seat belts save lives. You need to reinforce to your teenagers that setting rules is for their own good.

However, there are some absolute truths which, as a parent, you may want to convey to your children. Now whilst these are for the good of the young person, you need to understand that in today's culture there are no such things as absolutes, everything is relative. Such a statement is illogical but it's the way most people in our society live.

Josh McDowell writes that as parents you need to beware not to communicate the fact that certain truths are for the child's benefit but that they are simply right. He writes:

> $5 \times 6 = 30$ is not true because I get something out of it. It is right because it is right, because it reflects certain laws; it reflects reality. The point of offering evidence for truth to young people is not that the benefits or consequences of a belief or behaviour make that thing right or wrong, but that it can help them learn to distinguish right from wrong and of course choose that which is right.[37]

Setting boundaries has been a recurring theme. There are some issues for which you will only be able to set these boundaries as you go along, as the situation actually arises. But there are other areas in which you can be proactive, setting out guidelines for your family in advance of adolescence. Let me illustrate what I mean.

When my wife and I moved to Bromsgrove we were pleased to see a Woolworths in the town. We knew where to go to buy those stick-on soles for the home shoe-repair service. On the first occasion we went into the store we heard a mother telling her daughter who was about 3 years old, 'Come on we're going now. Come on we're leaving.' As the little girl carried on playing with the toys the mother's voice rose, 'Come on we're going now! If you don't come, I'll leave you!' We carried on looking for the things we wanted and spent about seven minutes in the store. For the whole of the time we were in Woolworths this monologue continued, 'Come on, I won't tell you again, we're leaving. I shall leave you here!'

When we left the mother was still there with her child. That 3-year-old had already learnt that her mother's word meant absolutely nothing. When she grows up to be a teenager, her mother may well wonder why her daughter takes more notice of her friends than she does of her. Making rules is an important aspect of parenting: it shows you care and it demonstrates your love. The problem is that rules are made to be broken, or at least negotiated! Are there guidelines for parents of adolescents? Well, the simple answer is, 'Yes' and here are some principles to help:

Get the most help and advice possible. Talk to other parents, to the parents of older children, to youth workers and teachers. Work hard to be sure that the boundaries you have identified are the right ones.

Involve the adolescents. It is amazing that when young people are brought into the discussion how fair and reasonable they seem to become and how fair and reasonable the punishments for breaking the rules become. In this way, when a rule is broken, you do not have to think of the sanctions on the spot with the possibility that the young person will declare them 'Not fair'. It is imperative that everyone is aware of the rules and the consequences. You need to be ready to negotiate and you must be committed to unity and consensus.

Work together. Don't give children the opportunity to play one parent off against another. This applies to two-parent families but where there is only one parent, children can learn to play off grandparents, especially where they have a significant involvement, against the lone parent. I shall be talking in more detail about lone parenting towards the end of the book.

Keep going. As you look into setting clear boundaries, you will find that new issues come up month by month that you hadn't even considered. To the obvious staying-out times, tidying of rooms, pocket-money levels, 'family together' times etc. will be added choices of magazines and videos, attendance at clubs and events, weekend sleepovers and parties, dating, membership of organisations . . . the list will go on and on. You will not need some form of parliamentary written rule for every one of these issues, but you will need some principles and procedures which establish from the outset that there are boundaries and that there are ways of saying what they are and sticking to them.

The more work you do on setting fair boundaries in pre-adolescent years, the greater will be the mutual trust and ease with which you operate through adolescence.

Those summertime blues

When it comes to making rules, don't they all fly out the window when examination fever strikes? I have been asked on a number of occasions about examination stress and if I have any advice on the subject. My first bit of advice is to avoid the problem we faced with our two sons. Our careful family planning not to have our children too far apart, resulted in there being exactly two years between them in school. This meant we were faced with A levels with the older one at the same time as GCSEs with the younger. I'm not sure who was under more stress, my sons or me.

I have also heard too often parents berating their children with words like, 'Look at what I've given up for you and you let me down like this!'

July and August each year are punctuated with similar exclamations from exasperated parents who failed to get their offspring to get down to study and are now facing the bleak future of daughter or son never getting a proper job. I certainly remember the trauma as if it was still only yesterday. The parched throat, the clammy forehead, the knotted stomach as the dreaded envelope came through the door. My school reports always said, 'Can do better', as though this would spur me on to greater things. It didn't.

So, as a parent, what do you do? Well, you can start making preparations now for when the moment comes; don't wait until your child has reached fifteen before instilling some good habits. I'm talking about your habits not the young person's. I've always thought character building to be on a par with academic success but try telling that to the parent of the child who has just flunked his GCSEs. That's why I'm telling you now, just in case.

Good habits for harassed parents:

1. Remember you're the best role model your adolescent can have. If you spend most of your time asleep in front of the TV, or uncommunicative in front of the computer, don't be surprised if they do too.
2. Make sure you affirm your teenager's good points, whether or not they are academic. All the pushing and shoving in the world will not work as well as the regular, 'Well done. I really appreciate you', followed up with a hug or a kiss.
3. Take an interest in what is happening to them throughout the exam period – ask about timetables and their particular worries. Try to reassure them rather than remind them that their whole future depends upon exam success.
4. Encourage a sensible revision strategy with organised breaks. Try not to nag as the days go by but by showing an interest you can gently check their progress and share in the process.
5. It is absolutely essential that you let your young person know early on that you will support them whether they succeed or not. This is the time to demonstrate unconditional love.
6. Listen carefully to what your teenager is saying about themselves and their own future, rather than trying to project your own desires onto them.

Habits to avoid at this time:

1. Now is not the time to attack their person. Never tell them they're stupid or a failure at any time, but during the run-up to exams, this can literally be fatal.
2. Now is not the time to say, 'If only you were more like your sister/brother'. Fortunately God made us all different. Also, don't tell them that they could do so much better if only . . . this wears them down.
3. Don't promise them things if they do well with their exams. They shouldn't have to work hard and achieve in order to feel this is the only way to gain your love.

4. Peer pressure is very strong for the teenager, so trying to ban all contact with friends during the exam period may seem a good strategy but it doesn't work. It's best to foster good friendships from an early age rather than rant and rave at the bad influences.

5. Do not feel guilty if your adolescent does not gain the level of passes hoped for. It's hard to realise but it is their life and it's the start of your letting go.

From my own experience as a parent in this whole business of examination success or failure, I can reassure you that even apparent failure can be turned to something positive. Both my sons failed to get the A level pass grades they needed for the university courses they had set their sights on. With James, our older one, we went through the trauma with him and learnt a lot about how not to handle the situation.

He was sure that Exeter was the university for him but he was refused a place. All our attempts to reason with him, to affirm him in the fact that he had achieved four A levels, and that there were still hundreds of courses open to him only resulted in a breakdown in communication. Fortunately a close and trusted friend of ours and of James, was aware of the situation. He was able gently to get James to look at the UCCA catalogue, along with those courses being advertised in the national press, and together they found a suitable course for him at Sussex University. He applied, was accepted and, even then, changed after the first year from Engineering with Business Studies to Computer Systems Engineering, a course which he loved. At the end he achieved a 'Desmond', a 2:2, and was justifiably proud.

With Andy we were prepared and when he too did not get on his first-choice course, we knew better than try and force him to look at the alternatives. We simply affirmed him in his passes, after all, four A levels are a great accomplishment. He also talked things through with a trusted friend, for he had observed the James débâcle and, after some telephone calls to the university he was accepted on a different course. It was the right one for him and it proved to be so by his achieving a 'First'. What proud parents we were at both their graduation ceremonies and all the trauma of those A level results was forgotten in the light of their degrees.

A student put it like this after her first year at university:

> Who am I to comment on the right choice of course as I have changed mine after the first year? However, I found that to pray about the decisions I had to make, whether they were major or minor, really helped. Also, listen to the advice and opinions of older people; like it or not, they often know what they're talking about. Enjoy student life and get involved in activities, they're the way to meet new friends.

Another student said:

> University is a place where you can live what you are; not what you have been in the past but how you want to be. I have found that I'm accepted much more as a Christian at university than I was at school and people respect me and see that my faith makes a difference to the way I live.

We have already touched on the question of withdrawal of privileges in the cases of rule breaking (Chapter 8: 'Conflict') but it is helpful to look at this question again in the light of making rules for the journey.

One mother told us she had grounded her son because she was fed up with telling him to bring his dirty washing to the kitchen. 'He is always leaving his boxers in his bedroom, no matter how many times I tell him.' I tried to explain that perhaps she should have thought through the punishment before handing it out and, whilst I believed in discipline, I also believed the punishment should fit the crime. Had she considered what her son would say to his friends when asked why he was grounded? Had she considered why he only seemed to have trouble with his boxers; his socks and shirts didn't seem to cause the same difficulty? What about giving him his own dirty-washing bag in his bedroom?

Dr James Dobson reckons that you discipline because it makes the child feel part of the family. He quotes the writer to the

Hebrews in the Bible, 'If you are not disciplined then you are ille-
gitimate children and not true sons and daughters' (Heb. 12:8).
He makes it quite clear that he believes in smacking children but
only for wilful defiance of the parent's authority and definitely
not after they are 8 or 9 years old. As your teenager's self-esteem is
in serious doubt in any event, a smacking is the ultimate insult,
making them feel like a child. As Dobson says, 'We want, then, to
shape the will of a child, but leave his spirit intact'.[38]

Many modern writers and experts will strongly disagree with
Dobson but at the annual conference of the National Association
of Schoolmasters and Union of Women Teachers held in 1998,
teachers mourned the loss of the parental 'wallop'. Parents were
criticised for treating their offspring like fashion accessories and
refusing to accept they could do anything wrong. The Education
Secretary, David Blunkett, said he would get 'tough as nails' with
bad parents. Parents it seems are more likely to wallop a teacher
who tells their child off than wallop the child!

Our research shows that the coming generation of teenagers,
the millennium generation, are the most wanted children in the
history of Britain. With the availability of contraception and
abortion almost on demand, parents are choosing to have children. They are another choice in the consumer culture. In just the
same way as people decide to 'have' a dog, they are deciding to
'have' a child. Many parents are not thinking through the consequences of this decision and just as a dog is not just for Christmas,
children are for life as well. However, the truth is many parents
choose to walk away from their children and the effects of divorce
upon teenagers is no less traumatic because they are old enough to
understand better what is happening. At the conference
mentioned earlier, a teacher said:

> Parents give their children everything they want and don't tell them
> off. Parenting is not saying, 'You can have everything you want and
> everything you do will be right'. Good parents take responsibility for
> their children in that they put on restraints and restrictions.

Chapter 15

Maintaining Communication

It is essential to do some creative thinking, in advance, as to how you will maintain open channels of communication. Don't assume that your child knows that you are available to talk, say so. Campbell has, as we have seen, some helpful advice on this subject and the discerning parent will learn to pick the signals up. A mother came to tell me, after one of the seminars, how she found that taking her teenagers by car was a great way to get them talking. 'It is as though they treat me like the taxidriver I suppose I am,' she said 'but they give me insights in the car they never seem to at home.' Make decisions in advance as to how you will organise your lives in order to spend quality time with your child through adolescence.

Creating support

Take a look around to see who is with you in the parenting task you face. This might include fellow parents, friends, relatives. Where there are people in whom you can confide, ask them to act as 'referees' for your family. Give them permission to blow the whistle on you when you need it, to warn you when things are going wrong, to gently chide you when you are at fault. If they are willing, ask them to become prayer partners with you in the mission of parenting.

Clearing out the rubbish

Whilst we have been concentrating on the things to pack for the journey, it is helpful at this stage to think of things that need to be cleared out the wardrobe and thrown away. Be prepared to face the issues in your own life that are thrown up when you think about adolescence. Many people have unresolved guilt, anger, disappointments, bitterness, fear and embarrassment dating back from their own journey through adolescence. You may need to give this some careful thought and even write some things down, so you can consciously deal with the issues. You may need to talk to a competent counsellor, or ask a friend to pray with you. If you are prepared to face the pain of 'clearing out the rubbish', you will be better equipped to accompany your child through adolescence, and better disposed to enjoy the experience.

From my own experience, I had to deal with the comments of my parents which dogged my self-esteem. I am the youngest of five children, with a brother, Michael, just less than three years older than me, and a gap of eight years to one of my sisters. Clearly my brother was a joy to my parents after so many years and, when he was born they decided to try for another child. However, my mother regularly told me, 'We only had you to be a friend for Michael'. That comment stuck in my unconscious mind until I was a parent myself and recognised the need to deal with it in order to help my adolescent sons better.

Praying it through

If you are a committed Christian, don't be afraid or reluctant to make the issues you have been looking at the subject of prayer. Your children matter very much to God, and the struggles you will face are real, not imaginary, but as we have already said, God knows what it's like to have a teenage son. Be ready to pray regularly during these years, to place your relationship with your child 'on the altar' and to seek God's daily help. If your situation allows you to do this with others, in a prayer triplet or group, all the better – you will be reassured and strengthened by the practice, especially if you pray with other parents and can share the joys and the challenges together before the Lord.

Conclusion to Stage 3:
Packing for the Journey

Key Points

Create a vision statement	For you as parent and for them as growing children.
Make rules ahead of time	Think through the issues.
Dare to discipline	'If you are not disciplined, you are not true children.'
Maintain communication	'My door is always open . . .'
Identify support	Who's in it with you?
Clear out the rubbish	Face your own fears and phobias.
Pray about it all!	Get help from the perfect parent!

A Challenging Diversion

Chapter 16

The Journey Through Single Parenting

This is a very important subject and, whilst I do not have space to give this issue the depth it deserves, I felt I should include a chapter to help single parents and those who care for them. In fact, I would recommend an excellent book written by Jill Worth and Christine Tufnell, *The Journey Through Single Parenting*,[39] for those of you wishing to know more. Christine Tufnell is also the founder of the Christian Link Association of Single Parents (CLASP) and the address is given in the Appendix. I attended a talk given by Christine Tufnell in November 1997 and found it very instructive. Here are some of the highlights of her talk and I am grateful to her for granting me permission to use them.

First a definition: 'Lone Parent' is usually referring to the parent who has day-to-day care of the child(ren). 'Single Parent' can mean this, but can also refer to the absent parent. 65 per cent of lone mothers have been married and are either separated, divorced or widowed. Only 9 per cent of lone parents are fathers. Before you rush into thinking that many teenagers are now lone parents, less than 5 per cent are under twenty years of age. By definition, one-parent families have a high risk of experiencing poverty.

There are many losses which lone parents have to face, including loss of partner/husband/wife, lover, provider, friend and often protector. There are more intangible losses such as trust, security, choice, hope and even the will and reason to live. They are on their own emotional journey and face all the parenting issues alone. For those of you in a two-parent situation, just consider for a moment what this means. They are responsible alone for the financial situation, dealing with all the bills, the bank, the Building Society and all too often the bailiff. Alone, they face their own emotional roller coaster together with their adolescent children (we are just thinking of parenting teens, but it applies to younger children too). Alone, they face the physical and spiritual changes in their children which we have already highlighted.

In spite of the loneliness, some single parents were positive in their comments. One mother said, 'I have a closer relationship with the children now. I love my independence and autonomy, not having to answer to anyone, making my own decisions, being in control of the finances.'

Another put it like this, 'I've found peace, the joy of new friends, less tension, no depression, much better health – I'm braver.'

Children of single parents experience bereavement, especially if a parent has died, but there is bereavement even when one parent leaves the family home. They also lose relatives and often friends as they have to move to a new home following the divorce settlement. Coupled with a loss of security comes the loss of innocence. Christine stressed that it was this latter point which hurt her the most, seeing her children having to grow up too soon. Another serious consequence is the loss of a role model, both the other-sex parent and the model of a good relationship between adults. Many children of lone parents maintain they will never get married themselves.

Children of lone parents also feel different. They feel betrayed and often guilty as if they, by behaving better, could have prevented the other parent from leaving. They have an overwhelming feeling of rejection and low self-esteem which results in behavioural changes over and above the ones discussed in this book. They withdraw from relationships of any sort, they regress into earlier childhood, become even more defiant than the usual youngster and are prone to emotional outbursts.

Obviously adolescents need greater understanding if they are facing all this additional baggage and the lone parent requires a

greater degree of support to see them through. In YFC we believe
the church is in a unique position to provide this support network
and we, the church, must be more sensitive to the needs of single
people generally, not just lone parents.

At this time, teenagers need honesty. It really is no good trying
to convince them that the other parent has gone on a journey, if
the truth is father or mother has died. Children can cope with bad
news given the right support and honesty from the start. Here are
some more needs of children of lone parents:

- Unconditional love (nothing new there)
- Respect for their views, their feelings and their desire to be
  normal
- Understanding of the real fears and concerns they are facing
- Security after a time when events have occurred which
  confused and changed their whole world
- Sense of self-worth
- Good and consistent role models
- Time for sharing about themselves
- Support before and after contact visits.

A teenage girl who did not have both parents at home, said, 'It
doesn't matter if you have six parents if they don't care. I'd rather
have just one that does.' I believe that any child who thought
about it could do nothing but agree with this statement.

Many of the people we speak to at the YFC parenting seminars
are facing the challenge of step-parenting. When one reads the
statistics published by the National Stepfamily Association, it
brings the situation into focus. Over 1 in 3 marriages currently en-
tered into in the UK ends in divorce. Over half of divorces involve
dependent children, around 450 children under sixteen every day.
Many people go on to remarry or live with a new partner, and so
create a stepfamily. It is estimated that by the year 2000 there are
likely to be between 2.5 million and 3 million children and young
people in stepfamilies in the UK.

The new marriage can have many permutations!

One partner could be: widowed, and/or
                               divorced
                               or previously unmarried
One partner could have: child(ren) living with them
                               contact with own child(ren)
                               no contact with own child(ren)
                               stepchildren living or not living
                               with them.

The other partner could be any of the above, or single and with no children.

This new marriage will be built in front of the children

There will be more pressures than for first marriages because of past history, because there is no time to build the relationship before the children come along and because often there is a lack of money. Coupled with this is the problem of housing the new family. Each of these elements is self-explanatory but there is no doubt that stepfamilies will require greater parenting skills than families where both natural parents are still together. In the view of Christine Tufnell, step-parenting has all the usual parenting issues, plus those of the single parent, plus some more.

It is good to know that, when reading her book, she has been through the challenges of divorce and remarriage with a new step-family and she speaks from a wealth of personal experience. She spoke movingly about this and how she and her second husband had coped with the situation and how the children of both families had learned to live together. She emphasised that success in this merging of two families was very dependent upon the quality of the relationship between the adults involved and the depth of their bond together.

However, in the Joseph Rowntree Foundation Report mentioned earlier, their findings relating to step-parenting were not so encouraging. The Report states:

There are many adjustments that children whose parents separate may have to make, most obviously that of no longer living with both parents. If their parents subsequently form new partnerships, they may experience a further transition into a household comprising one birth parent, another adult and, sometimes, stepsiblings. Research findings for children from stepfamilies suggest a number of ways in which they do not fare as well as those from intact families and, in some instances, not as well as those from lone-parent families. The risk of adverse outcomes for young people in stepfamilies compared with those in lone-parent families appears higher for older children, especially in areas of educational achievement, family relationships and sexual activity, partnership formation and parenthood at a relatively young age. Young children in stepfamilies seem to fare better, possibly because it is easier to adapt to a new family structure at an age when they have had a relatively short period of living with either both or just one birth parent.[40]

Christine Tufnell's own experience is that for the children it was also a moving experience in more ways than one. Such marriages will signal the end of any possibility of the child's parents getting together again and often result in moving to a new home. The desire to be 'normal' like any other family will be strong but parents entering into such a marriage need to be aware of the problems which the adolescents of the families coming together will face. Several people have spoken to us at the parenting seminars who are facing these types of challenge; some have found reasonable success whilst others are unfortunately struggling with the consequences.

One couple told us of the joy they had found in their new marriage and how their children had been the means of bringing them together. Their teenagers were best friends, both sharing the hurt of parental divorce and who had, unwittingly, acted as matchmakers. Here the challenge of loving another person's child was readily accepted and just as readily received. Rivalry and jealousy between offspring who were becoming siblings were largely absent. However, I have to say this is an unusual story. Mostly those we speak with are finding it really hard to bring two families together.

On one occasion a mother shared with us her real concern following a remarriage. She knew her husband really cared for her daughter but bringing him into the family had raised again his pain at not having day-to-day contact with his own children. He was having to work through this unexpected additional problem in the new marriage. For the teenager of that family there was the additional problem of learning that adults do not have their lives 'together'.

We have also listened to parents where a number of children have come together under one new roof. All the usual sibling rivalries are exacerbated. In the new family the oldest from one side was now somewhere in the middle, whilst the youngest found themselves no longer in this position. The difficulties did not end there. Each parent brought a different attitude to discipline which simply did not cross their minds in the days of planning for their new home life. The cries of 'It's not fair!' came thick and fast. All the damaging nursery rhyme tales of the wicked stepmother came flooding into the equation.

Christine Tufnell listed the following skills as essential to make step families work:

- Lots of love
- Time
- Patience
- Determination
- Building a relationship with each child
- Respect for the individual
- Understanding
- Support and encouragement
- Blending into the new family
- Finding one's own role within the family
- Good (that word again) couple relationship
- A sense of humour
- Above all, parenting skills

Someone has said that the stepfamily can be a productive and satisfying family, though its form is different and complex. (We haven't even touched on the subject of grandparents!) Step-parenting is the hardest job in the world and the one with the least training. A primary school teacher said, 'What makes such a difference to the child is not the number of parents, or their legal relationship, but the parenting skills and loving relationships of those they live with.'

Alys Swan-Jackson writes of the accounts of adolescents with whom she spoke regarding step-parenting:

> The teenagers who contributed to this book who got along with their step-parent best agreed that they were like a good friend, i.e. someone who could give them help or advice, provide a shoulder to cry on and perhaps even share hobbies and interests with. As a friend, the step-parent could criticise and give advice but they didn't assume the authority of a parent.[41]

With so much going against the chances of success, organisations such as CLASP are very valuable in supporting stepfamilies but so should the church. Unfortunately, too many of the people we have spoken with have found the church's attitude to remarriage both unhelpful and often downright antagonistic. We must show a greater love and understanding to all those who are working to be good parents of teenagers, whether we are individuals, neighbours, friends, or church.

Death and separation

I hope it will be helpful to mention that research into the effects of parental death and parental separation show different outcomes. I want to handle this as sensitively as I can, for I want to be practical for those of you who may have experienced the trauma of the death of a partner and to be wise in helping others who may find themselves facing such a situation. To blandly quote from a report will not be very helpful but my purpose in writing this book has been to help you prepare for this business of preparing to parent teenagers and some of you will have to face this very real issue.

At the end of the film *Shadowlands*, staring Anthony Hopkins and Debra Winger, there is a very moving scene just after Joy Gresham has died. C. S. Lewis, who had married Joy, is in the attic of his home talking with Joy's son, Douglas. Not much is said in their shared grief. They simply hug each other and weep together. Man and boy mourning.

Immediately prior to this scene, Lewis' brother had urged Lewis to talk to Douglas and although Lewis had felt he did not know what to say, it was good advice. As in divorce, it is natural to try to protect children from facing up to death, but all the evidence points to the benefit of honesty and openness. Let C. S. Lewis from his own account in *A Grief Observed* give some advice.

> I was happy before I ever met H [Joy Gresham]. I've plenty of what are called 'resources'. People get over things. Come, I shan't do so badly. One is ashamed to listen to this voice but it seems for a little to be making out a good case. Then comes the sudden jab of red-hot memory and all the 'commonsense' vanishes like an ant in the mouth of a furnace.[42]

C. S. Lewis was trying to be honest about his grief but at the same time to be helpful to others who walked the same road. He had a stepson to look after and a demanding job as professor at Magdalen College, Oxford and wanted to avoid the slippery slope of self-pity. By facing up to his situation he helps us to understand a little of what it felt like for him and, as a result, to be in a better position to help our children cope with the death of a parent. The report I mentioned earlier produced by the Joseph Rowntree Foundation, says:

> Children from separated families and children who have experienced the death of a parent share the impact of parental loss and the

longer-term experience of parental absence (more often of fathers than mothers). Research suggests that bereaved children are adversely affected, but not across the same range of outcomes as children whose parents have separated. In particular, parental death does not carry the same risks of poorer educational attainment, lower socio-economic status and poorer mental health. There is evidence for an impact of bereavement on some behavioural outcomes in childhood and adolescence, including substance use and leaving home at an early age, but these do not appear to persist as disorders in adulthood.[43]

Conclusion to A Challenging Diversion

Key Points

Single parenting is not easy	But there can be good outcomes.
Children of lone parents feel different	They need honesty and loving support.
A new marriage is built in front of the children	But it can work.
Step-parenting is the hardest job in the world	With the least training.
Learn the skills which make step-parenting work	Lots of love, time and patience.
If there is death and separation	Remember to communicate honestly.

Stage 4

The End of the Journey

Chapter 17

Independence – The Final Frontier

One of our workers found this witty quote in her sons' hairdresser's:

Teenagers! Tired of being harassed by your stupid parents?
Quick! Leave home, get a job and buy a house while you still know everything.

Contrary to what you may be thinking, or even perhaps, hoping, the transition from adolescence to adulthood and leaving home, does not happen instantaneously. The moment you have dropped her off at college or university is not the moment she is independent and an adult. Nor does the moment he gets his first full-time job mark completion of the development of teenager to adult. As Dr Ross Campbell puts it: 'The transition into adulthood should be a gradual weaning process for which both parents and teenager prepare.'[44]

At a question time during one of the parenting seminars a parent commented that we made the business of parenting teenagers sound like a full-time job. 'I want a life', she said. Just at the time when you may be thinking you can get your life back, here I am saying it's not over yet. I hope I haven't made it sound like a full-time job but, to quote Michael Howard again, 'Parenting is a process which goes on to when you are a grandparent'.

Two of our friends tell us of the dramatic time when their youngest daughter ran away from home at the age of seventeen. I have included their story as a help and support to those of you who may have to face this at some dreadful time. I hope what they say will be of comfort to others who have been through this particular mill.

She writes

The background to our youngest child disappearing was unhappiness at work, and not realising how desperate she felt, we encouraged her not to leave until she had found something else to go to.

Nothing could have prepared me for that day. A note was left in the kitchen saying 'Sorry for everything and goodbye'. After checking her room (nothing much seemed to have gone), and phoning work (she hadn't arrived), panic began to set in. My stomach was churning. What should I do first?

I phoned the police even before my husband and, because of the note, two policemen were on the doorstep within fifteen minutes. They asked so many questions covering every area including child abuse, family arguments etc. They wanted to keep the note and asked if we would mind publicity if it became necessary. These sorts of things never happen to us – it's what you read in the newspapers or see on television.

I didn't want to tell my mother because she is quite unwell and it would upset her so much, but I had to. There was a small group of people I wanted to tell, not because there was anything they could do but I knew they would pray. The rest of the family were wonderful. Friends came round and we decided on various places she might be. They went out and searched all day.

My husband and I did not voice all our fears. I could hardly speak anyway but individually we were imagining all the awful things that might happen. I just prayed that God's angels would surround her from all the evil and dangers that she might come across.

That day was so long – we couldn't eat but we drank a lot of tea. As the evening came, our thoughts went to her spending the night out in the open – where? How would she cope? The phone had rung on and off all day and each time we wondered if it was possibly good news.

She rang at about 6 o'clock from somewhere in London, in tears and feeling cold and miserable. Thank you God for keeping her safe. Then I recalled that in the morning, before I went to work I had put my head round her bedroom door and said that I hoped she would have a good time at the theatre (with the girl from work) that night and if she needed a lift home from anywhere, she just had to call us. I'm so glad that I had said that.

He writes

It is always something that happens to other people – not you. It just doesn't happen in Christian families. The big question that revolves with the monotony of the gyroscope is WHY? The fact that you cannot find an answer doesn't stop you asking. You begin to focus on all the occasions that you felt highlighted your inadequacy as a parent. It was because you only scored six out of ten in the Parenting Advice book and it must be the other 40 per cent that is the reason.

We spent some time working out what we should do – we needed a plan of action. The horrible realisation dawned – there was not much we could do but wait. What was so hard was that you felt so much emotion but there was no constructive way of channelling it. We had no idea where she was and all we could do was wait. We asked God in our prayers, between sobs and tears to bring her to her senses and prompt her to come home, but if she chose not to, at least to keep her safe and free from harm and danger. We had spent 17 years caring for her, providing all her needs (or so we thought) but she appeared to have other ideas.

We started to think back to recent times when we had said (or not said) certain things. When was the last time I had told her I loved her? After seven hours of mental agony, the phone rang. 'Hi Dad, its me. I'm in London but I've got no idea where.' These became the most marvellous words I had ever heard. The rendezvous was arranged and the return home effected. Relief and joy drained us so much that running the marathon would have seemed a far easier option![45]

Perhaps it would be helpful to see how young people themselves see this period of transition. One 19-year-old talked of the time he went to university.

> I didn't appreciate mum and dad till I went to university. When they phoned up we never talked so much. Mum even hugs me on visits. She was stand-offish before.

There is no doubt that living away from home does change the relationship between children and parents. Some parents find it much easier to relate to their children as they get older and, if you have been preparing them to establish their own identity, you will be able to relate to them as adults without difficulty. The letting-go aspect is important. I know of parents who found it really difficult to do this and visited their daughter on the second weekend she was at university. This did nothing for their daughter's street credibility. As I have said many times before, the preparation for this time is invaluable so you are ready for when it actually happens. It involves not just you as parents, but your daughter or son as well.

Here are some helpful points to consider:

1. Practice runs

The teenage years are a good time to introduce opportunities for your teenager to spend periods of time away from home. Summer camps and events such as 'Soul Survivor' are excellent ways of preparing your teenager for full independence. Having taken our church youth group to both Stoneleigh Bible Week and 'Soul Survivor', I can recommend them as safe places for older adolescents to gain experience in looking after themselves.

A few of the older members of the group volunteered to work at Stoneleigh and came back full of the enjoyable times they had, together with a real sense of achievement. They had been empowered to accept responsibility and demonstrated that they could be trusted – demonstrated, I guess, as much to themselves as to anyone else.

Our son James volunteered to work with YFC during two of his summer vacations. It would have been good if he had been able to supplement his income but, at the time, holiday work was very scarce. He spent his summer cleaning loos and serving at tables and learned to share his faith with those who came to the 'Fort Rocky' weekends (special weekends run by YFC at Pioneer Centre) where 11- to 14-year-olds had the opportunity to hear about Jesus. He was at 'Fort Rocky' when his A level results came through.

Andy did 'Street Invaders' where YFC takes over 100 young people and trains them in how to share their faith. They then go onto the streets of a town or city to put their new-found skills into action. It was at 'Street Invaders' that Andy became courageous enough to come back and tell his school friends that he was a Christian.

Don't just take my word for it, here is an extract from a letter received in August 1998 from one parent:

> Our daughter recently returned from 'Street Invaders'. She said it was the best two and a half weeks of her life! She has been much encouraged and her faith has grown since being part of this worthwhile ministry.

2. Increase self-sufficiency

Having two sons meant that it would have been easy to gender stereotype them and keep them out of the kitchen. Val did not allow this and, as part of the preparation for independence, made sure both sons could cook and do their laundry. James has never progressed beyond the tin-opener and microwave but he did realise that if he bought a packet of biscuits he could eat them in one sitting and they were expensive; on the other hand, a bag of carrots lasted a lot longer! He was also smart enough to land the job of House Manager in the student lodgings he had in Brighton. Not only did he get reduced rent for doing this but he could organise his fellow students to rent a washing machine thus negating laundry problems! He maintains that he even ironed his T-shirts! When we were talking about this book, he was quite insistent that I should state he even taught his wife to use the washing machine and iron shirts as she had never been shown by her parents. James is the only student I know who finished university without an overdraft. No wonder the minister at his wedding called him a skinflint.

It is important that you prepare your teenagers so that they understand about a balanced diet and are capable of buying the necessary ingredients to satisfy the full range of the body's needs. If you have always done everything for them they will find it almost impossible to fend for themselves when they have to. I am sometimes surprised to speak with older adolescents who do not know what actually goes into every student's basic meal of chilli con carne!

3. Money matters

By the time your adolescent becomes independent he should be able to handle his own finances. This means that you will have to train him in budgeting and balancing his money. It is also a good idea to have helped your child to handle their own bank account. Whilst this may seem a fairly trivial matter, you will be surprised how many young people I had to help with this when I was a bank manager. The discipline to put money aside as savings is no longer the norm for most adults, let alone young people. I remember well my days with NatWest Access where we had the slogan, 'Access takes the waiting out of wanting'.

Most banks will be trying to attract your teenager's account with offers of cash gifts, free travel cards, free credit cards and free overdrafts. Unless they know how to deal with money, teenagers can fall into serious debt and financial difficulties which will live with them for many years.

One young man came to me in my capacity as bank manager. He was a member of my church and I hoped to be able to help him out of his financial mess. I asked him to let me have a breakdown of where he spent his money. He simply could not tell me. I suggested we went through his cheque book stubs but he didn't bother to keep a record, nor did he retain the slips when he withdrew money from the cash dispenser. As a next step I wondered when he had last balanced his bank statement and he admitted to never checking it as it was always so depressing! In order to assist this young man I had to insist, as a first measure, that he kept a record for three months of every penny he spent.

It seemed to work. He is now married, with a mortgage and the responsibility for a small child. I know his parents were not uncaring but the lessons about money had not been learned. Habits which last adults through their whole lives are often shaped in older adolescence. As I have said repeatedly, teenagers are not adults and whilst their characters and emotional make-ups have been largely formed during this period, they can still be changed. As parents you can make use of this time when they are gaining independence to reinforce the good ones and, hopefully, change those that are not so desirable.

4. The family left behind

It is true to say that mothers are more affected by the departure of children from the home than fathers. It was certainly true in our house. Val found it really hard when we moved to Bromsgrove. She had been working as an occupational therapist but the move meant she had to resign. I had a job which I was finding fulfilling but Val had an empty house, no friends and no sons. It was an unusual situation in that we were the ones who had flown the nest! We have never managed to rebuild it so that James and Andy felt it was home.

This has resulted in Val having to go weeks, sometimes months without seeing either James or Andy. The situation was exacerbated when James got married. His future wife's parents were wonderful, doing all they could, at a distance, to involve us in the preparations. But, we were in Bromsgrove and they were in Surbiton. We couldn't simply pop round for a cup of coffee. It was a great occasion thanks to the planning of James' in-laws, but I know Val would have loved to spend more time enjoying the build-up.

Parents aren't the only ones affected by the departure of daughter or son. Younger brothers or sisters can also find the new arrangement difficult. Here are some comments from younger siblings.

> I suppose I've got closer to my parents now my sister's left and I'm the only one. But I find it annoying and claustrophobic as I'm an independent person.

> It was hard losing Debbie as a friend. Being left behind bothers me. I hate school when I'm seeing others doing what I really want to do. I get more attention but sometimes it gets a bit much.

They also needed to adjust to the new situation and many felt that they were being smothered and it would be harder for them to leave when their turn came. For some the changes were positive: 'Life at home is more relaxed', someone told us. It's impossible to know what will happen when the children start to leave home but it is part of life and part of becoming an adult. I know from my own experience that treating my sons as adults has been a learning experience for me and I asked them how I had done. I'm sorry, their answers are not to be published!

I think it is all too easy for us to believe our children no longer need us once they have made the first step into independence. If you think this, it is a mistake. The security you as parents offer remains a vital part of their lives, for their needs emotionally have changed little since they were children. Dr Ross Campbell puts it like this:

> Even at this stage, they need to know that we genuinely love them, that we are available, and that we will help them in any way we can, for their own good. As long as they feel we truly care for them, we

can continue to have a constructive influence in helping them achieve independence.

However, the most important anchor of security a teen leaves behind is the marital relationship of his or her parents. One of the most devastating things that can happen to an adolescent soon after leaving home is the separation or divorce of his or her parents. It's as though the foundations of his whole world are crumbling. Yet, it is amazing how many parents actually plan to 'stay together for the sake of the kids, but as soon as they leave home, we're getting a divorce'.[46]

I know it sounds unreasonable but the young person will feel that she is responsible for the bad marriage and divorce. If you are desperately holding together a marriage that is heading for separation as soon as the 'kids leave home', it is far better to make the break, with her full involvement in the process, before she leaves home. In this way the adolescent's natural feelings of loss, guilt and grief can be worked through with friends prior to the task of leaving home which will have enough trauma of its own.

It was fascinating to watch a family of blackbirds using our garden to fledge their young. The parent birds never seemed to stop for a moment collecting food for their young; it made me quite exhausted just watching. Within a very few days it was quite clear the adult birds decided that the youngsters were capable of fending for themselves and they quite deliberately drove the now fully-fledged birds off their territory. This is a picture of good parenting and whilst it may seen a little drastic to drive our young people away, we can do so with full confidence, if we have done all we can to equip them for the 'outside world'.

Chapter 18

The Last Word

Faith, hope and love: and why you'll need all three!

We have already looked at the need for unconditional love in all your dealings with your teens. It hardly needs repeating that love comes before, after and during all the suggestions contained in this book. Love must be the ground you work from and the material you work with. It is worth remembering, when love is at times strained, that 'loving actions create loving feelings'. At times when it is hard to feel love for a person close to you, the answer often lies in demonstrating love towards them, and letting the feelings follow.

I shall never forget the panic when my second son was born. Would I have enough love to go round? I loved my wife and our first son so much that I was really troubled that this new member of the family would somehow get short shrift in the love stakes. It was as though love could be sliced up like a cake and found wanting. Of course my experience soon showed that love is not a commodity to be portioned out and kept for when the occasion demanded, but real love does not run out.

Faith and hope are also needed because in your moments of panic and disappointment, you need to know that God is just as committed to your success as a parent as you are. Whatever dreams and visions you have for your child he has more. He is on your side and at your side, available to you at every moment. In addition you need to know that you are not solely responsible for the outcome of your parenting efforts. You have a very important part to play as we have explained but your children themselves have their part to play. And in the end you must not carry a burden of guilt if your efforts seem to have failed. Remember, Adam and Eve had the perfect parent but they still messed things up!

Anne Frank, writing as a teenager herself shortly before her death in a Nazi camp, said this:

> I'm beginning to realise the truth of Father's adage: 'Every child has to raise itself.' Parents can only advise their children or point them in the right direction. Ultimately, people shape their own characters.[47]

The last and most important skill you will need in parenting is trust. Trust, built on faith and hope, is what will keep you from despair, will energise your efforts and will make parenting not a solo task, but a partnership between you, your child and the God who loves you both. Trust is such an important component of any relationship but with teenagers you must show an increasing willingness to trust. Be sure the time will come when your adolescent will come and say, 'Dad, can I borrow the car?'

When my younger son learned to drive I was ready with the reply to the question. I was driving around in a company car, it was an automatic, fuel-injected, two-litre Sierra and he had learned in a small Nissan with a manual gear box. Furthermore, the first £500 of any damage was down to me and I could not afford this risk, bearing in mind the difference between my car and the one he was familiar with. He nodded understandingly and accepted the position. Phew!

A couple of weeks later he came again, 'Dad, can I borrow the car?' I rehearsed the well-thought-out argument. 'The car's different, is more powerful than you're used to, has an automatic gear box and the first £500 of damage is down to me.'

My son had also been rehearsing his response. 'Well Dad, you know I've been saving for ages, but if I were to buy a car it would cost more than £500 and the insurance alone would be at least that amount on top. I tell you what, I'll pay for the £500 excess if I damage the car and you'll be saving money!' I handed over the keys. How could I refuse such logic and effrontery? The problem was I was so taken aback by the conversation I forgot to stipulate a time for him to come home.

At 11.30 p.m. we went to bed. By midnight I was still wide awake. By 1 a.m. there was still no sign of him and I had looked out the window at the sound of cars goodness knows how many times. By 1.30 a.m. I was beginning to panic. My wife was trying to remain calm and pretend she was asleep. Just then the car drew up and I was ready to give him what for: how dare he stay out this late, keeping us awake and showing no consideration whatever. Then I remembered, I had not agreed a time for him to come home and he was simply being a teenager. I had showed I trusted him but now I needed to explain, in the morning, that when he borrowed the car I wouldn't be able to sleep until I knew he was safely at home. We always agreed a time from then on, and he never abused it.

And finally . . .

In 1996 the General Synod Board of Education jointly with the National Society and Church House Publishing produced a report called 'Youth a Part' in which tribute was paid to parents. We feel this should act as the epilogue to this book:

> This report cannot be written without paying tribute to and emphasising the vitally important role played by Christian parents. They are there in their role of mentors, teachers and supporters of young people during the years when their faith is developing and becoming a first-hand 'faith of their own'.[48]

So often, in practice, it is Christian parents who support the youth worker, who encourage their son or daughter to attend events, who act as chauffeur to hordes of young people. They may end up late at night providing a 'sounding board' to other people's children as they prop up the kitchen table or sit on the stairs. The partnership between parents and the more formal 'youth worker' can be creative and supportive especially where the parents are sensitive to the needs of young people. It is important for many parents to know that the youth worker, who may be mentor and confidant to their son or daughter, is working from a base of Christian values.

The parents' role is vital in the life of a young person. The integrity of the parents' lives and faith has a crucial influence on young people.

Appendix 1

Useful Names And Addresses

Christian Link Association of Single Parents
Linden
Shorter Avenue
Shenfield
Brentwood
EssexCM15 8RE

Hope UK
25f Copperfield Street
London SE1 0EN

Care for the Family
Garth House
Leon Avenue
Cardiff
CF4 7RG

Soul Survivor
7 Greycaine Road
Watford
Herts
WD2 4JP

Spring Harvest
14 Horsted Square
Uckfield
East Sussex
TN22 1QL

Notes

Preface

1 Piper, Colin, *Families: Don't You Just Love Them!* (Farnham: CWR, 1994)

Chapter 2

2 Mandela, Nelson, *Long Walk to Freedom* (London: Little, Brown and Company, 1994) p. 25
3 Gilbert, Pete, *Understanding Teenagers* (Nottingham: Crossway Books, 1993) p. 58
4 Lowe, Gordon, *The Growth of Personality* (Harmondsworth: Penguin Books, 1985) p. 164
5 *Daily Mail*

Chapter 3

6 Dobson, Dr James, *How to Build Confidence in Your Child* (London: Hodder & Stoughton, 1997) p. 38
7 *Ibid.*, p. 49
8 Campbell, Dr Ross, *How to Really Love Your Teenager* (Aylesbury: ALPHA, an imprint of SP/Valley Trust Ltd, 1997) pp. 44, 45

Chapter 4

 9 Campolo, Tony, from an exclusive interview, the full text of which is available from YFC
10 Short, Claire, *Parenting Teenagers* (Milton Keynes: Scripture Union, 1996) p. 21

Chapter 6

11 Gallagher, Michael Paul SJ, *Clashing Symbols* (London: Darton, Longman & Todd, 1997) pp. 7, 8
12 Toffler, Alvin, *Future Shock* (London: Bodley Head, 1970)

Chapter 7

13 Chalke, Steve, *How to Succeed as a Parent* (London: Hodder & Stoughton, 1997) p. 139
14 *Ibid.*, p. 141
15 Gregory, Ian, *No Sex Please, We're Single* (Eastbourne: Kingsway Publications, 1997) p. 42
16 Short, Claire, *op.cit.*, p. 69
17 *Ibid.*, p. 70

Chapter 8

18 Extracts and Articles from the *Methodist Magazine* published in 1802
19 McDowell, Josh, *Right from Wrong* (Milton Keynes: Word Publishing, 1995)
20 *Drugs, A Parent's Guide* (Booklet produced by the Department of Health, 1992) p. 4

Chapter 9

21 Hickford, Andy, *Essential Youth* (Eastbourne: Kingsway Publications, 1998)
22 Cohen, David and Gaukroger, Stephen, *How to Close Your Church in a Decade* (London: Scripture Union, 1992)
23 Collins, Gary, *I believe in the Family* (London: Hodder & Stoughton, 1996)
24 Campbell, Dr Ross, *op.cit.*, p. 70
25 *Ibid.*, p. 79

Chapter 10

26 Blair, Tony, during the Prime Minister's speech at the Labour Party Conference, 1997
27 Abrams, P, 'Social Facts and Sociological Analysis' in P. Abrams (ed.) *Work, Urbanism and Inequality* (London: Weidenfield and Nicholson, 1978) p. 10
28 Report obtained from the Joseph Rowntree Foundation, Web Page (www.jrf.org.uk, 1998)
29 Swan-Jackson, Alys, *Caught in the Middle* (London: Piccadilly Press, 1997) p. 102

Chapter 11

30 Quoted in *Tackling Bullying in Your School*, Sonia Sharp and Peter K Smith ed. (London: Routledge, 1994) pp. 2, 3
31 *Youth a Part*, Published 1996 for the General Synod Board of Education jointly by the National Society and Church House Publishing with funding from the Department for Education and Employment
32 Sharp, Sonia and Smith, Peter K., *Tackling Bullying in Your School* (London: Routledge, 1994) p. 96

Chapter 12

33 Peterson, Eugene H., *The Message* (Colorado Springs: NavPress, 1993) p. 386
34 Williams, Margery, *The Velveteen Rabbit* (London: William Heinemann Ltd. 1988) p. 17

Chapter 13

35 Campolo, Tony, from his interview with YFC
36 Parsons, Rob, *The Sixty Minute Father* (London: Hodder & Stoughton, 1995)

Chapter 14

37 McDowell, Josh, *op.cit.*, pp. 125, 126
38 Dobson, Dr James, *op.cit.*, p. 105

Chapter 16

39 Tufnell, Christine and Worth, Jill, *Journey Through Single Parenting* (London: Hodder & Stoughton, 1997)
40 Report obtained from the Joseph Rowntree Foundation, Web Page (www.jrf.org.uk, 1998)
41 Swan-Jackson, Alys, *op.cit.*, p. 88, 89
42 Lewis, C. S., *A Grief Observed* (London: Faber and Faber, 1981) pp. 7, 8
43 Report obtained from the Joseph Rowntree Foundation, Web Page (www.jrf.org.uk, 1998)

Chapter 17

44 Campbell, Dr Ross, *op.cit.*, p. 144
45 Dent, Kingsley and Margaret, used with permission of all the people involved.
46 Campbell, Dr Ross, *op.cit.*, p. 151

Chapter 18

47 Frank, Anne, *The Diary of a Young Girl* (London: Viking, Published by the Penguin Group, 1997) pp. 326, 327
48 *Youth a Part*, Published 1996 for the General Synod Board of Education jointly by the National Society and Church House Publishing with funding from the Department for Education and Employment, p. 85

Bibliography

Abrams P., Social Facts and Sociological Analysis in P. Abrams (ed.) *Work, Urbanism and Inequality* (London: Weidenfield and Nicholson, 1978)

Campbell, Dr Ross, *How to Really Love Your Teenager* (Aylesbury: ALPHA, an imprint of SP/Valley Trust Ltd, 1997)

Chalke, Steve, *How to Succeed as a Parent* (London: Hodder & Stoughton, 1997)

Cohen, David and Gaukroger, Stephen, *How to Close Your Church in a Decade* (London: Scripture Union, 1992)

Collins, Gary, *I believe in the Family* (London: Hodder & Stoughton, 1996)

Dobson, Dr James, *How to Build Confidence in Your Child* (London: Hodder & Stoughton, 1997)

Frank, Anne, *The Diary of a Young Girl* (London: Viking, Published by the Penguin Group, 1997)

Gallagher, Michael Paul SJ, *Clashing Symbols* (London: Darton, Longman & Todd, 1997)

Gilbert, Pete, *Understanding Teenagers* (Nottingham: Crossway Books, 1993)

Gregory, Ian, *No Sex Please, We're Single* (Eastbourne: Kingsway Publications, 1997)

Hickford, Andy, *Essential Youth* (Eastbourne: Kingsway Publications, 1998)

Lewis, C. S., *A Grief Observed* (London: Faber and Faber, 1981)

Lowe, Gordon, *The Growth of Personality* (Harmondsworth: Penguin Books, 1985)

Mandela, Nelson, *Long Walk to Freedom* (London: Little, Brown and Company, 1994)

McDowell, Josh, *Right from Wrong* (Milton Keynes: Word Publishing, 1995)

Parsons, Rob, *The Sixty Minute Father* (London: Hodder & Stoughton, 1995)

Peterson, Eugene H., *The Message* (Colorado Springs: NavPress, 1993)

Piper, Colin, *Families: Don't You Just Love Them!* (Farnham: CWR, 1994)

Sharp, Sonia and Smith, Peter K., *Tackling Bullying in Your School* (London: Routledge, 1994)

Short, Claire, *Parenting Teenagers* (Milton Keynes: Scripture Union, 1996)

Swan-Jackson, Alys, *Caught in the Middle* (London: Piccadilly Press, 1997)

Toffer, Alvin, *Future Shock* (London: Bodley Head, 1970)

Tufnell, Christine and Worth, Jill, *Journey Through Single Parenting* (London: Hodder & Stoughton, 1997)

Williams, Margery, *The Velveteen Rabbit* (London: William Heinemann Ltd, 1988)

Other papers and publications

Daily Mail

Extracts and Articles from the *Methodist Magazine* published in 1802

Drugs, A Parent's Guide (Booklet produced by the Department of Health, 1992)

Report obtained from the Joseph Rowntree Foundation, Web page (www.jrf.org.uk, 1998)

Youth a Part. Published 1996 for the General Synod Board of Education jointly by the National Society and Church House Publishing

Burghes, Louie, Clarke, Lynda and Cronin, Natalie, *Fathers and Fatherhood in Britain*, Occasional Paper 23, Family Policy Studies Centre, 1997

A Guide to Family Issues, Family Briefing Paper 2, Family Policy Studies Centre, October 1997

Care for the Family, Factsheet 2, Divorce, 1997

Crime and the Family, Conference Report, Occasional paper 20, Family Policy Studies Centre, October 1994

Roll, Jo, *Young People: Growing up in the Welfare State*, Occasional Paper no. 10, Family Policy Studies Centre, 1990

Divorce and Separation, Summary Document of full report by Bryan Rodgers and Jan Pryor, Joseph Rowntree Foundation, June 1998

Family Policy Bulletin, Summer 1997, Families and Education, Family Policy Studies Centre

Tackling Drugs to Build a Better Britain, Government White Paper, The Stationery Office, 1998

Unpublished material kindly given to the author by Colin Piper and Christine Tufnell

Scripture quotations are from the New International Version of the Bible (1973, 1978, 1984 by the International Bible Society)